ead All About It...

ong last is coming true!

Speedway

BIG CAR

between Philadelphia and Trenton.

31

Time Trials 1 p.m.
First Race 2:30
6 - BIG EVENTS - 6
25-Mile Feature

JOHNNY THOMSON

ands of race fans this will be the first
ne, the world's fastest circular mile track.

ast and many from the midwest in ac-
0 miles an hour on the world's fastest

eserved) $2.50 Plus Tax. First Come, First Served.

The American
Dirt Track
Racer

Joe Scalzo

94

MBI Publishing Company

Dedication
For Bruce Craig, Bob Mount, and the spirit of Ronnie Allyn

First published in 2001 by MBI Publishing Company, 380 Jackson Street, Suite 200, St. Paul, MN 55101-3885 USA

MBI Publishing Company books are also available at discounts in bulk quantity for industrial or sales-promotional use. For details write to Special Sales Manager at Motorbooks International Wholesalers & Distributors, 380 Jackson Street, Suite 200, St. Paul, MN 55101-3885 USA

Library of Congress Cataloging-in-Publication Data Available
ISBN 0-7603-1017-3

On the front cover: Al Unser; Sacramento; October 4, 1970. Bob Tronolone

On the frontispiece: Elmer George; Sacramento; October 16, 1961. *Bob Tronolone*

On the title page: Bill Homeir and Cotton Farmer; Sacramento; October 25, 1959. *Bob Tronolone*

On the table of contents page: Parade lap, Sacramento; October 29, 1961. *Bob Tronolone*

On the back cover: [Top] Parade lap, Sacramento; September 28, 1969. *Bob Tronolone*
[Mid Right] Jim Hurtubise; Sacramento; October 25, 1959. *Bob Tronolone*
[Lower Right] Colby Scroggin, Don Branson, and Bobby Marshman; Sacramento; October 28, 1962. *Bob Tronolone*

Edited by Kris Palmer
Designed by Dan Perry

Printed in China

Contents

Chapter 1

1951–1971

THE PANZER AND THE FLOWER CHILD

The Panzer

It's 1962—the 11th season of 1951–1971's banner binge of dirt track racing—and another great year to be alive.

Three-quarters of all championship car, sprint, and midget combat takes place on dirt, so the righteous dirt track message covers the continent from East Coast to left coast, all through the Midwest, the far Northwest and East, even, on occasion, the taxicab stocker Deep South. Everything's jamming—exploding—with magic and overheated racing and there are platoons of amazing race drivers, herds of mad characters, packs of fascinating race cars, and a terrific menu of astounding race tracks, including the sun-blasted Arizona State Fairgrounds in Phoenix, which is my destination.

Three hours ago, when I exited the city, Los Angeles was still in darkness, but now dawn is lighting up Interstate 10 as my butterscotch Monza Corvair with trick reverse-chrome wheels and hundred-pound sack of Redi-Mix in the nose—the only way to plant the fly-away front end—hurtles and swerves toward beautiful Blythe, the Colorado River shantytown on the California-Arizona line where worrywart Indianapolis car owner Bessie Lee Paoli once had to be hospitalized overnight to repair her bleeding ulcers. Keep mashing the pedal and avoiding highway patrol heat, I tell myself, and I'll hit Phoenix in time for hot laps on the mile track.

Mile tracks! The most venerated of all dirt theaters, in addition to Phoenix, they include the Illinois State Fairgrounds in Springfield and the same state's other mile at DuQuoin; the Indiana State Fairgrounds in Indianapolis; the New York State Fairgrounds in Syracuse; the California State Fairgrounds in Sacramento; and, finally, the most fearful of all, Langhorne Speedway in rural southeastern Pennsylvania.

Heroes of the Tony Bettenhausen/Jimmy Bryan/A. J. Foyt class always expect to maul and dominate miles the same way they do everyplace else, but miles are diabolically uncooperative when it comes to laying down and getting pancaked flat and lifeless. Giving a stiff upraised middle finger to the heroes, they fight back by exploding into ruts, ridges, and holes—the nastiest of which hide in the dust and launch heroes into sky or fence.

Miles, then, are old-fashioned punishment palaces, and Phoenix's is one of the best/worst. Persecuted by gruesome Arizona summers and rainless winters, the parched and hardpan fairground's mile annually comes in not with dust clouds but dust storms, and not with mundane bumps but horrible craters. Not surprisingly, Phoenix 100-milers sometimes get red-flagged and have all racing interrupted so that maintenance crews can take desperate shots at bandaging the blown-up surface.

One Sunday Phoenix 100 that dispensed even more than the usual mayhem was 1954's, which murdered

At the beginning of the 1951–1971 era, Tony Bettenhausen was dirt tracking's premier player. And he was going strong almost a decade later, as he was here at the 1959 Sacramento mile. Everybody wanted Panzer Tony's services.
Bob Tronolone

Spectators along the front straightaway at the Phoenix mile got to experience the sensation of having big dirt champ cars almost in their laps. Then in 1962 they got more than they bargained for when Elmer George in his careening *HOW Special* entered the main grandstands and went into the seats—literally—somehow with no really serious injuries to anyone, not even Elmer. *Bob Tronolone*

eight of its 18 starting cars in the opening 35 miles. A 24-hour time-out was called and everything put on hold so that the 10 pitiful semicrippled chugs left in the race could be revitalized with fresh shocks, spindles, or whatever; so that their 10 battered drivers could get first aid and, hopefully, regain their senses; and so that the whole monster track could be lobotomized by giant 'dozers attacking the sonofabitch all night long.

Monday's restarted match was won in a typical rout by colossus Jimmy Bryan and his white-and-blue Kuzma, the mighty *Dean Van Lines Special*, the most famous car in dirt sport. Yet without the crisis measures, Phoenix that year might well have achieved a

mile's ultimate fantasy of rising up, devouring *everything*, and having *no* finishers at all.

Watching all this Phoenix carnage season in and season out is, admittedly, a guilty pleasure. Not a pleasure to see beautiful race cars and hero drivers take a bludgeoning, but to feel goose bumps while observing the heroes rip into their roles as masters and start doing tricks with their lurching, bucking, solid-axle Kuzmas, Meskowskis, Watsons, and Kurtis-Krafts. Chasing a ruined mile-track groove from top to bottom lane and back again . . . picking out cornering patterns that straddle trenches . . . putting arms and souls into keeping control and bouncing and roughhousing from rut

What racing. Rough-track combat on the ragged Phoenix mile could rip a steering wheel from a driver's grasp, or pop a champ car out of gear, but wasn't supposed to be crash 'n' burn. Rodger Ward ignored this rule in his disintegrating and airborne *Leader Card 2*, coming in for a bone-jarring landing in 1961. Championship mile-track racing in its classic age was demanding of an all-action technique: knowing how to exploit an angry and unforgiving race track without trashing the race car. *Bob Tronolone*

Phoenix mile pace lap, 1957:
Rodger Ward and his Springfield/
Sacramento-winning Lesovsky, the
Walcott Special, and Johnny Boyd in his
Kurtis-Kraft roadster—an Indy 500 car
on dirt!—the *Bowes Seal Fast*, outside.
Jimmy Bryan and the unstoppable *Dean
Van Lines* Kuzma broke down a
crashwall and still won. *Bob Tronolone*

to rut, making crash-landings without crashing—mile-track racing is an art. A. J. Foyt is, for me, the all-time greatest at such action, but before A. J. came Phoenix homeboy Bryan, and before the two of them came the Panzer: Tony Bettenhausen.

Terrible Tony was in some ways even better than Bryan and Foyt. What he really was—even though none of us in dirt track racing knew what the word meant, or what you did with it—was charismatic. Monumentally so. With piercing eyes of two different colors, he looked as if he wasn't quite of this world. And because a rough-track idol ought to be a rough guy, so Tony could be, and it wasn't a pose. "By God, if it's fighting you want, let's get to it!" he once declared, blissfully setting off an afternoon of fisticuffs at a road-house. Racing, he regularly had his race cars roaring at everybody else's, and other drivers realized what hell was like when Tony Bettenhausen was bearing down from behind, demanding right-of-way privileges; for additional intimidation, there was Tony's occasional habit of delivering a hard nudge to people he passed. Yet Tony was a full-on enigma, too, because there were

two of him: first, Tony Bettenhausen the husband and father, courteous gentleman, good friend; and second, Tony Bettenhausen the fiend incarnate race driver ready to hit you a ton.

Pre–World War II, Tony developed his chops as the youngest, most aggressive torpedo among a hot tribe of midgeteers from John Dillinger Chicago who raided and pillaged and plundered and raised the roof every-where from Soldier Field to New Jersey and the dreaded velodrome of decapitations at Nutley.

From there, Tony grew into the ogre of champi-onship racing on dirt, especially rough dirt, at the clas-sic 100-mile distance. The whole American Automobile Association cavalcade briefly fell under his domain when the Meyer-Drake consortium, maker of the Offenhauser, tapped him to chauffeur a midget that had been stretched to accommodate a screaming experimental Offy with a supercharger on top. But fol-lowing two Tony runaway wins in a row, all Meyer-Drake customers were ready to mutiny unless M-D parked both car and Tony. So M-D compromised by retiring the engine but turning over everything else to a well-heeled sportsman and Bettenhausen fanatic named Murrell Bellanger.

It was 1951, and Tony and his earth-mover *Bellanger 99*, a Kurtis/Lesovsky, were slammin'; winner of eight of the campaign's 12 mile meets, Tony made a farce of the national point standings. The trouble was, what could he possibly do for an encore? So much of him had been used up dominating this one pedal-to-the-metal tournament that for the next three seasons he existed in a sort of off-again/on-again retirement.

Then, in 1954, Tony was in the process of winning another main event—not in a big Offy but a popgun 110 midget—when he dropped his guard and climbed a wall, fracturing his skull. Perhaps he came back too soon, but he said race cars were his only medicine. Besides, he was out to show any skeptics that, busted melon or no, by God there ain't nothing the matter with Bettenhausen!

However, 1954–1957 was the era of Jimmy Bryan, and nobody, including Tony, could get in big Jimbo's way, so it wasn't until 1958—seven long campaigns after Tony's bellwether 1951—when Tony found the opportunity to get his old status back. At age 42 he became the senior participant in a gigantic brawl with the formidable likes of Johnny Thomson and Jud Larson for the U.S. Auto Club points title, USAC by now having supplanted the extinct 3-A as dirt racing's idiot tyrant sanctioning body.

As usual, the year's 100-mile wrap occurred at the Arizona State Fairgrounds, and even by Phoenix standards was a thriller/chiller. Tony boomed off the outside of the second row to go into the lead, but the dominant dandy on the mile that afternoon was Jud Larson. A fantastic loafer and beer hound when not in a race car, yet faster than anybody when the spirit moved him, Jud repassed Tony and flew high for 30 miles, until hearing a fresh Offy opening up just behind. Glancing over his shoulder expecting to see Tony, Jud instead found himself staring straight into the fierce kisser of Eddie Sachs, who, when racing on dirt, twisted his face into a Halloween horror mask. Sachs had no stake in the title fight, but was going to make trouble anyway, and one look at Eddie's contorted puss caused Jud to evacuate the area in fright. Blowing into lapped traffic and throwing off a blizzard of trademark Larson broadsides, he made spectacular pass after pass keeping ahead of crazed Eddie.

Meanwhile, back in fourth behind Jud, Eddie, and Johnny Thomson, Tony was feeling frustrated. The

Grand old warrior Tony Bettenhausen never laid down on the track and raced joyously hard. Even when he got to be twice the age of kids trying to beat him he wouldn't slow down. He took losses to heart and dispensed no favors. Bitterly disappointed after losing the 1960 dust bowl Syracuse 100 by just 10 feet, he came out to Phoenix to make up for it. But he ran over an exposed wheel, hit the outer steel rail, then pinballed back onto the track and collected three cars, two of which flipped. Nothing personal; it was just the all-out way Panzer raced. *Bob Tronolone*

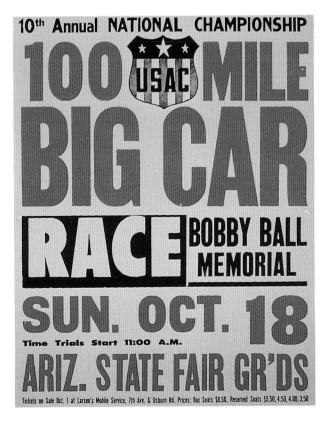

10th Annual NATIONAL CHAMPIONSHIP
100 USAC MILE
BIG CAR
RACE BOBBY BALL MEMORIAL
SUN. OCT. 18
Time Trials Start 11:00 A.M.
ARIZ. STATE FAIR GR'DS
Tickets on Sale Oct. 1 at Larsen's Mobile Service, 7th Ave. & Osborn Rd. Prices: Box Seats $8.50, Reserved Seats $5.50, 4.50, 4.00, 3.50

Year in and year out, the infamous Phoenix mile ran a near dead-heat with Langhorne as the mile dirt track from you-know-where. *Bob Tronolone*

Arriving at a mile track early when its surface was still prime and fast was a must. Otherwise you'd miss hot laps and not get to see those drivers with the heaviest feet backing 'em in. This is Chuck Hulse in the *Dean Van Lines Special*, Sacramento 1963. *Bob Tronolone*

Phoenix dirt carpet had again turned into the Phoenix minefield—there were two particularly big holes in the first corner and another at the entry point of No. 3—and the three idiots ahead of him were getting away. Presumably muttering his all-purpose battle mantra of, "My head says no, but my foot says *go*!/My head says no, but my foot says *go*! . . ." Tony wound himself up and unleashed the most dependable of all appendages: the Bettenhausen foot of lead.

Soon he was smeared all over Jud, Eddie, and Johnny. Then he went to work overwhelming them with textbook underside and topside attacks that carried him up, down, and across Phoenix's rim, middle, and bottom.

Nobody could take that kind of wasting pressure forever, but initially fighting back the hardest was Sachs, an agitated wheelman under the best conditions. However, a 20-mile dose of Bettenhausen torture made Eddie spin his car back to front and call it a day. Thomson caved next. And Tony continued prancing.

With 25 miles to go, Larson still led with Tony camped out just behind, preparing to apply the Bettenhausen tattoo. Jud had other ideas. Catching some terrific shots off the fourth corner to extend his advantage, Jud got racing so fast that Tony or nobody else could hold him. Tony being Tony, he went on trying in spite of slow-down signals from his pit crew, which he ignored until his overworked engine got sick.

Runner-up in the Phoenix 100, Tony was nonetheless first in the standings and winner of the national title. Then, in 1959, he took a flier at another seasonal championship and, even though he didn't quite pull it off, proved that he still had it by winning Phoenix outright.

Back in real time, I'm still heavy-duty on the button for Phoenix when there's a sharp yelp of engine, a carnival of warning lights on the dashboard, followed by stony silence. And I'm sitting stranded in the hell-'n'-gone outside of Blythe with an utter loss of power.

My little Monza, in protest of my honking pace, has gone bananas and flung its air-pump belt off the pulleys. That's the least of it. The wayward belt has wrapped itself around the distributor cap, wiping out all timing and electronics.

Extricating myself from this fix makes it impossible for me to make Phoenix on schedule, and I have to turn around and limp home to L.A. This is fortunate, because I'm able to miss witnessing Phoenix's greatest disaster yet. In a dozen 100-milers, the unforgiving fairgrounds mile has routinely smashed the life out of its

Tony Bettenhausen's 1959 Phoenix-winning *Lindsey Hopkins* Kuzma gets a workover. *Bob Tronolone*

champ cars and occasionally even its race drivers, yet one thing it has never done previously is give a hammering to its paying spectators—until 1962. There's a wild scene on the front straightaway when for some reason Elmer George punts Ralph Ligouri's *Windmill Truckers Special* in its tail and then Elmer's *HOW Special* swerves right and sends eight people to the fracture ward by entering the main grandstand and going upside-down in the crowd!

Fast Time

The last blast of summer for the big champ cars is the Indiana State Fairgrounds—and, baby, if you want to make some of that fat bread the Hoosiers pay at their Hoosier Hundred match you'd better have your hoof well in it when you go out and time trial. In 1955 Edgar Elder does. The first qualifier to set wheels to the prime surface, Edgar and his *Ernie Ruiz Special* go balls-out and earn prestige by setting quick time for the day.

Edgar's father was an all-world motorcycle trigger, also one of the co-inventors of the Harley hog-derived Drake midget car engine, but Edgar himself isn't a wheelhouse man of high reputation. He's won pole position at the Hoosier Hundred because of the luck of the draw—literally.

If you're a race driver at the Hoosier Hundred and everywhere else, you don't get to warm up, put your box in the qualifying line, and say, "OK, I'm ready, let's go." Instead, you have to draw a number out of a hat. Draw a low number, as Edgar did, and you get the race track when the dirt's smooth and choice. Draw a high number and go out after several other sleds have torn things up and little race track is left, and you'll post an abysmal time and earn yourself a starting post at the caboose. Worse, mile tracks (except Langhorne) draw more

entrants than can be accommodated—30 or more teams bickering over a mere 18 starting holes—so maybe you'll miss the show completely.

Shafted by the ill luck of the draw, the likes of Bettenhausen, Larson, Sachs, Rodger Ward, and sometimes even Foyt all occasionally missed starting mile shows during 1951 to 1971. A. J., in fact, may have invented the not-very-sporting practice of reaching into the hat and grabbing a whole fistful at once. But I can't recall ever seeing phenomenal Don Branson not qualify for a mile-track race, and it didn't matter how savage the surface was. At Sacramento alone Don won three poles, including 1966's, when he exploded everybody's mind: 22nd of 25 drivers to qualify, and with the outside cushion reduced to marbles, he leaped onto a strip of undisturbed dirt that nobody else wanted any part of and rode it to quick time.

Following Bettenhausen up the line of succession as dirt track colossus was Jimmy Bryan. Whether on the craters of Phoenix and Langhorne, or the iron surface of Syracuse, or anywhere in between, big Jimbo won. Dirt tracking took plenty of steering, and Bryan's mighty Kuzma, the *Dean Van Lines*, was built deliberately roomy for its animated muscle-man operator to jump about in its cockpit for 100 manic miles.
H. F. Bergquist, Scalzo collection

1

2

Edgar Elder and A. J. Shepherd weren't alone in having their difficulties with the Hoosier Hundred. In 1954, the *Bob Estes*, an automobile built in collaboration by A. J. Watson and Jud Phillips, took a wild journey courtesy of its driver Don Freeland; Don emerged unscathed. With their champ car a wreck, A. J. and Jud a couple of days afterward carried their *Estes* sprint car to a meet at Ft. Wayne. And had it get wadded, too. *Hollingsworth-Greiner, Stew Reamer collection*

Don had authority and smarts, knew all about tires, traffic, and tricks, and yet he was also stooped, baggy, infirm, and a bit of a grumpy old coot. The reason Don stood so mercilessly on the gas when he qualified wasn't to show off for the crowd: it was because he wanted Foyt, Hurtubise, Parnelli Jones, and other younger, stronger studs to be starting behind him. That way he didn't have to wear himself out trying to pass them in the race.

It was a mystery how he managed to, but Branson always looked smooth, even while breaking a track record. By comparison, many of those aforementioned studs like A. J. Shepherd—yet another A. J.—could panic your heart.

A soulmate of Parnelli, Hurtubise, and Jack "Upside-Down" Rounds who'd boondocked, barnstormed, and spectacularly rim-rode all around the International Motor Contest Association, A. J. Shepherd arrived at the 1961 Hoosier Hundred and made a happy discovery. His canary-color *Bell Lines Trucking*, honchoed by Buster Warke, the chief mechanic and Offenhauser wizard, was a rocket; in hot laps, A. J. was fastest of all drivers.

"They'll not catch *this* yellow sumbitch today," A. J. advised Leroy Neumeyer, ex-salt rod chauffeur and another old dirt pal. Giving himself the ol' needle, A. J. went on, "We got pole!"

"If the race track lets you," replied Leroy, attempting to talk A. J. down. But A. J., alas, was w-i-r-e-d. By the bad luck of the draw he didn't get to time-trial until 16 qualifiers ahead of him had already taken big greedy mouthfuls out of the surface and reduced the dirt to junk.

Going for it anyway, A. J. disappeared headlong into turn one with Buster's *Bell* going at full bark. A. J. snapped the steering wheel hard left, the *Bell* hooked a rut, and the rut made it head for and then hit the railing and next leave the race track doing end-over-ends. Outside were barns and stockyards to whack—the Indianapolis Fairgrounds and most of its brother miles were designed not for champ cars but four-legged nags and trotters—and whack them the endo-ing *Bell* did. Afterward, A. J. was sentenced to three months in crashhouses having his broken body rebuilt and replumbed. Buster Warke, by comparison, lived the hard culture of a chief mechanic: he had a month to rehabilitate the mangled *Bell* in time for Sacramento, plus he had to lasso some new chauffeur.

Edgar Elder's 1955 chief mechanic and sometime race car constructor is Wally Meskowski, a hard-boiled, I've-seen-everything type who, like Buster, is accustomed to cleaning up the messes and mistakes of race drivers; Wally, too, will end up with a heavy restoration job instead of a Hoosier Hundred pole. Edgar Elder, you see, never returns from his pole-winning ripper! On what is supposed to be a cool-down lap, Edgar instead continues pedaling and makes the lame move that turns into an "Oops!" and his *Ruiz Special* jumps so high that it brings down 40 feet of fence, two cement posts, and stops with its wadded-up nose pushing into the concrete of a third.

The Hoosier Hundred's quick-time automobile never even gets to race—not even I've-seen-everything Wally Meskowski has ever seen anything quite like this.

Tommy Meets Jud

It's 1956. Let's imagine that I'm some dork paying my first visit to Pennsylvania and the crucible playpen of Reading, sprint car racing's centerpiece of rim-riding. I scarf down the castor oil smell, investigate all the 220 Offys, especially the hot Sam Traylor jobs, and look over Jiggs Peters, Charlie Musselman, Al Herman, Johnny Thomson, etc., who're strutting their stuff and preparing to set up for business. But after checking out all those hammer-down heavy dudes, I can't take my eyes off somebody else. Curiosity at last gets the better of me, so I go to some of the Reading insiders seeking the identity of the hog-jawed horticulturist in the baggy coveralls with the gut on him who's working on the blue sprinter.

Back comes the reply, "Oh, that's Tommy. He's this old farmer they let be a gofer and stooge."

The answer satisfies me until I notice something else. "Hey," I protest to the same Reading insiders, "you know that old farmer guy who's a mechanic? Well, he's putting on a helmet and climbing into the car!"

So the insiders blandly reassure me, "Aw, they just let him warm it up until its real driver gets here."

Yeah, right. The next thing that happens, the hammer drops, an Offenhauser gets blasting, and the grandstands jump out of gear roaring with excitement as "Tommy" starts jumping around in the cockpit traveling nine million miles an hour across the rim top. Watching his hands endlessly clubbing and tomahawking the steering wheel lock-to-lock makes me stop breathing.

Gullible moron that I am, I've just bitten on the Tommy Hinnershitz hoax, perhaps dirt racing's oldest dumb-guy gag, and one that Reading regulars love pulling on visiting idiots. But the same insiders now tell

Setting sail across mile-track grooves, Don Branson, dirt racing's great grandpa, seemed to improve instead of decline with age. In 1966, his last tour of action, he won the Springfield 100, Terre Haute's midget classic the Hut Hundred, and on the Sacramento mile made a fast-time qualifying lap on an impossible surface that will be remembered for as long as anyone fortunate enough to have seen it is still alive. *Bob Tronolone*

me not to get sore, but to get ready. Hot laps are a yawn compared to old Tommy careening and blasting real estate clear out of Berks County while passing a pleasant Sunday afternoon doing a violent rim job for all eight or nine minutes it takes to win another Reading 20-lap feature.

Torching Reading with that runaway, tomahawking style of his, Tommy sometimes even bicycles onto two wheels—he's the busiest-looking driver going. And à la Tony Bettenhausen, Tommy's a split personality, a real Jekyll-Hyde. Take him out of his *Miracle Power Special*—a flyaway midget/sprint car crossbreed, like most

P-A jobs—and Tommy's that benign medic, Jekyll: a weathered, paunchy, middle-aged Pennsy-Dutch sodbuster living with family and cows on the Hinnershitz back 40 over in Alsace Township by the river Schuylkill. But plant Tommy in the *Miracle Power* and he'll do the big Hinnershitz switcheroo and turn into crazy Mr. Hyde defending Reading/Allentown/Williams Grove as if they were medieval fortresses.

Having Peters, Musselman, Thomson, and the rest of Pennsylvania's dirt posse piling in on him season after season is competition enough for Tommy. But, courtesy of an oversized dirt track celebrant named

Samuel A. Traylor III, this 1956 campaign has turned into one of Tommy's toughest ever. Big Sam (he stands 6-feet 4 inches and goes around 260) is a piece of work. The original Traylors made their first pretty buck in mining, and later in Allentown erected an enormous pile that Pennsy chronicler John O'Hara occasionally writes about called the Traylor Hotel; but Sam's own contribution to family honor is ownership of the flashiest race car scuderia in the East. Earlier this June, Sam had imported celebrity Pat Flaherty, the Indy 500 champion. Ordinarily a non–sprint car driver, Pat imagined that 20 laps against Tommy Hinnershitz at home was going to be as diabolical as 200 around the Brickyard. But while Tommy was upstairs, Pat was busy working the bottom; in a huge Hinnershitz defeat, and team Traylor upset victory, Pat had waxed Tommy slicker than hell.

Now it's October at Reading, and big Sam has imported someone else capable of racing at the rocket tempos Tommy likes: the jalopy desperado and Los Angeles maniac Van Johnson.

But on what will turn into an afternoon for the ages, Tommy sees another dangerous invader sliding up—a lackadaisical tumbleweed and saloon cowboy named Jud Larson. Fresh from an earthquake showing at the Hoosier Hundred, Jud's got the infamous *Pfrommer Offy* all loaded, and it's pointed straight at Tommy.

Jud zaps turns one and two without lifting, comes low into three in another four-wheel broadslide, then aims the *Pfrommer* to the top of turn four and finishes up with a signature Larson slide-for-life clear to the timing stripe. Quick time! In fact, a new Reading track record!

Jud and Van Johnson both make hard moves on Tommy, then take off together in the feature. They go to war. But then Hinnershitz, not content to be the goat, and all hooked up himself, adjusts his attack and nails the pair of them dead to rights off turn two.

Johnson fades but Jud goes after Tommy. All Larson broadslides have a hypnotic will-he-spin-out? quality— they seem to go on forever, and Jud keeps throwing them. It's strictly a Hinnershitz-Larson race. They ride high against the rail in one and two then cut and chop across the middle down in three and four. They're missing

It's been nice, boys, but I'll be seeing you! Tommy Hinnershitz, outside, checks out on Van Johnson, middle, and Jud Larson, inside. Terrible Tommy raced sprint cars in a frenzy. He had a full-blown horror of any surface but soil, a racing range of only 15 miles (each one hair-raising) and a simple formula—go to the rim and stay there. Better than anyone else over east at Reading and Williams Grove, Tommy could get a sprinter flying so fast it bicycled up on two wheels, yet bring it back into control without crashing. *David G. Knox, Scalzo collection*

His fantastic racing stable included three sprinters, a midget, and a dirt champ car, making big Sam Traylor the majordomo of Reading, Williams Grove, and 1950s' eastern racing generally. His employees included, left to right, Johnny Thomson, Eddie Sachs, and Van Johnson. Sam also liked to make sure his shoes gave it the old college try: "Listen, you losers, my race cars are the fastest in the country. So are you going to stand on it or stroke? What's it going to be?" Yet nobody was ever badly hurt in a Traylor sled. *Bruce Craig*

one another by inches and there's no room for error: whenever Tommy appears to be hopelessly trapped or blocked, he sets himself free with an astonishing swerve or impossible veer that Jud immediately duplicates.

Following nine fantastic minutes spent pointing out holes in each other's repertoire, they hit the finish blanketed. But Tommy's driving was fractionally better and he has won again. All hell pops loose from the grandstands—even by Reading standards this was one stunning war—and when Hinnershitz and Larson halt side by side on the front straightaway, Tommy looks typically placid, Jud, for once, dazed.

He'll next return to the premier mile tracks of the national championship and discover that first-place paychecks against Bettenhausen and Bryan and the demigods come easier than they do against stay-at-home Tommy. Throughout 1956–1958, Jud will capture more 100-milers than anybody but Johnny Thomson, and who knows how many more he'd have won but for racing with a hangover after getting smashed the night before? However, he's learned his lesson and will seldom be returning to Reading to take on Tommy. "That old hayshaker's got eyes in the back of his head," Jud moans.

Jud Larson was loose, totally flaky, and so relaxed that he sometimes appeared to be falling asleep at the wheel while breaking all four tires loose and serving up the most radical and dazzling broadslides of the period. *David G. Knox, Scalzo collection*

Above and opposite: Jud performed his signature slides not just in three-quarter-size sprinters on the half-miles, but in the monster dirt champ iron on full miles: just poke it down in turn one, eyeball the most inviting piece of cushion, snap everything sideways, and stand on the gas. Nothing to it. *Bob Tonolone*

Surprise! Surprise!

It's 1959 at Sacramento, and although the 100-mile champ car matches are the best races in dirt tracking, the penultimate round here is frequently the national tourney's sorriest.

Everybody's dreading the coming rough-track hell of the Phoenix finale. Worse, it's fall, another season is expiring, and as usual things are coming unglued. Drivers are either quitting car owners and going to new car owners or else drivers are getting pink-slipped by car owners and the same is true of all the other elements of the floating menagerie of champ car combat including stooges, roadies, and chief mechanics. With so many teams in the process of going dead in the water, everybody is feeling burned out instead of racy.

But marching across Sacramento's green grass pits with his German shepherd comes this warm-hearted and wisecracking visitor from outer space with large-bore eyes winking like high-beam headlights. Seeing them, Jud Phillips, the race-worn chief mechanic, thinks to himself, "Uh oh. Wally Campbell eyes."

Wally Campbell was the ill-starred jitterbug with ray-gun orbs who'd earlier and similarly arrived—though not at Sac—by surprise and put the squeeze on racing. Troy Ruttman had called him the most radically talented race driver he'd ever seen, but just when he was threatening to grow more rad, Wally was in a mysterious crash in the *Nyquist Offy* followed by a three-story fall into a corn field, climaxed by an explosion and fire.

So who's this strange new bird with the fire eyes? He's Jim Hurtubise, soon to become "Hercules," "Herk," "Herkie," "Herkie-bear," and similar endearing monikers invented to honor him, his eyes, and all the mad stunts that will make his dirt career constantly hair-raising. Opportunities open up unexpectedly in dirt racing, and, just a couple of months before Sacramento, Herk had been off in IMCA sticks, raising all kinds of podunk sprint car fury. Then Johnny Thomson had gotten hurt again and the champ car wheelhouse of the *D-A Lubricants Special*, Johnny's renowned Kuzma, opened up. D-A Lubricants had decided to give rookie Herk a shot, hiring him for the Hoosier Hundred. Unfortunately, some of the same referees and sanctioning body powers-that-be who five years earlier had been spooked by Wally Campbell now were put off by Herk; before gaining permission to race at the Hoosier Hundred, he was forced to jump through hoops and take a hazing. So after not doing well at the HH, and then bombing in his next two shows, too, here he is at Sacramento, ready to surprise at last.

Tommy Hinnershitz's near-nemesis Jud Larson was one of those recommending Herk, but Jud can't be at Sac to watch Herk's coming surprise because at this moment—something like Johnny Thomson—Jud's himself in sick bay getting patched up from the wear and tear. Jud really should be at Sacramento, too, because he's the originator of this whole big surprise business.

It happened back in banner year 1956. Having spent most of his life avoiding having to *race* for a living— except for a disastrous stint with the high-and-mighty 3-A who suspended Jud as a good-for-nothing—and objecting to having to *work* for a living, Jud's latest general delivery address was Kansas City, where he was coining halfway decent dough bartending as well as broadsliding hardtops, midgets, and sprinters at Olympic Stadium. He won continuously, except at the race when his midget had all its instruments peg, and—not knowing what-from-shinola about nuts and bolts—raced merrily on as oil and raw fuel from the dying mill filled his boots. At last the engine went up in flames, along with Jud's boots and feet. Nothing but huaraches felt good to his tender toes afterward, so naturally he bartended wearing them. And won all the Olympic races in them.

Then, through a fluke, Jud got assigned the *John Zink No. 8*, the reigning national champion automobile, and was sent to the Hoosier Hundred.

He showed up in a T-shirt, holding a dilapidated crash hat with a hole in it, and wearing those same huaraches. Accustomed as they were to working with Indy 500 winners and other big weenies, all the Zink mechanics including A. J. Watson gazed in disbelief at their surprise pilot: how in the world had this yokel slipped under the radar and even gotten into the pits?

When Watson skeptically asked him how he wanted *No. 8* set up, and Jud told A. J. to set it up to run first, Watson thought Jud was blowing smoke. But Jud wasn't: he earned pole with virtuoso broadsliding, or, in Jud-speak, "runnin' it into the corners backward." Saying sayonara in the race was going to be impossible, of course, because nobody there was about to permit a visiting vagabond like Jud Larson to ace the Hoosier Hundred. Outside of winning Langhorne, which carried a whole different sort of prestige, the Hoosier Hundred—with prize money second only to the Indy 500's, and with most of the big teams headquartered right in Indianapolis—was the circuit's crucial 100-miler.

So the race began and Jud split. Just like that. Jimmy Bryan had started right next to him, and ordinarily Bryan had the ability to go as fast as he could go the moment a race took off. Yet Jud continued leading anyway. Racing exactly as he'd qualified—with endless broadslides mile after mile—Jud gapped the great Bryan by a straightaway at mid-race.

Jud's style *was* Jud. A big, slow-moving blond with a big, slow laugh, he spoke laconically through a Tex-Okie slang and treated racing as a means to avoid working. *Bob Tronolone*

Running far behind, Tony Bettenhausen, committed to trashing Jud for the sake of esteem, instead got frustrated and drilled a fence. Johnny Thomson spun out. Jud, in other words, was making everybody go crazy. Jimmy Bryan tried not to go crazy and his persistence paid off. Jud jinxed himself by slapping his diamond sidewalls so hard against the outer cushion lap after lap that he almost obliterated it, leaving himself nothing to race on, and pounding his car to the breaking point. Finally, the *Zink No. 8* had the right rear suspension collapse. After Bryan's savvy chief mechanic Clint Brawner awakened Bryan with a message on a blackboard and set Jimbo on Jud, it was all over.

Even in a crippled car, Jud still achieved an honorable fourth place. Bryan and Brawner saluted Jud's big surprise by taking him with them for beer call at everyone's favorite house of spirits, the White Front, where, like a good sport, Jud joined his new friends in sucking down cool ones into the wee hours. (Not too long after this he set out on his unsuccessful Reading rendezvous with Hinnershitz.)

Like Jud in that shock showing, Hurtubise was ready to surprise the field at the 1959 Sacramento. Maybe Jud could sense it in recommending that Herk be allowed to compete. He only qualifies a so-so 11th. But then Eddie Sachs flames a piston. And Bettenhausen loses a magneto. Now the race track comes to Herkie and he goes nuts lapping the field. Surprise! Surprise!

Mudbath

Skittery-jittery 110 Offys always put on the tightest races, and the majority of dirt soldiers—including A. J. Foyt, who will race midgets almost 150 times—continue campaigning them long after they'd become established big shots in champ cars and sprinters. Midgets are a reliable means of picking up some fast scratch, and what a rush to race without touching the brakes and to kick your pygmy sled sideways and get those doughnut tires fanning a rooster tail of race track into the grandstands!

A full-blooded midget has teeth, and of course some of the brand names will get bitten—Andy Linden critically, Shorty Templeman and Jimmie Davies fatally. Midgets, though, are mere toys compared to champ dirt cars of almost twice the tonnage and 3-1/2 times the ordnance. Paradoxically, after 1951–1971 concludes, certain connoisseurs will argue that maybe the most dominating driving effort of the 20-year dirt orgy wasn't put up in a champ car, or even a sprint, but a midget.

Curiously, roughly two months prior to Jud's surprise showing at the Hoosier Hundred, that same superb 1956 season produced another great surprise, this one on the blood-red mile at Atlanta. Unfriendly Atlanta—right in the heart of NASCAR door slammer territory—was a dangerous oddity banked on one end and not the other, and with a start/finish line so close to the first corner that champ cars frequently struck the crashwall. Which is what happened on the 99th mile, when the leader, Fatty Veith, misread a pit signal and had to glance back to reread it. When Fatty was back looking straight again he was already raising an atomic cloud of red dust overrunning the first corner and battering Atlanta's wall. The starter of the race went hysterical at the sight of Fatty's spill, let the race go another lap, then waved the red flag instead of the checkered. Swirling off the last corner, dueling for the lead, came the *Sam Traylor Special* of Al Keller and the second-place *Lee Glessner* of Eddie Sachs—here depicted years after in 1961 in the *Dean Van Lines*. Eddie was a mile-track novice and hugely unpopular motor-mouth who'd only gotten the Glessner chauffeuring assignment that morning, yet ended up as Atlanta's totally unexpected winner. Surprise! *Bob Tronolone*

It occurred in the frozen fall of 1961: raw and bitterly cold Terre Haute, a western Indiana racing community that's going to be the future site of Elmer George's final downfall but right now is fairly forlorn except for its celebrated cathouse and its even more celebrated half-mile named the Action Track. But the 10th annual Hut Hundred classic, ordinarily first- or second-rated as the most prestigious of all buzzbomb scrambles—the Turkey Night Grand Prix on the coast was the other biggie—has "disaster" scribbled all over it.

An appalling mess, the devastated surface of the Action Track is so slow and awful at the beginning of time trials that all early qualifiers, including Foyt—who missed by just one tantalizing car—don't go fast enough to make the 36-midget starting cut. Then the maintenance dummies overwater the thing and make Terre Haute a soggy swamp. All heat race eliminations get cancelled while trucks and tractors spend the late morning and early afternoon slithering and sliding and attempting to groom some sort of race track. They fail. Goo and mud notwithstanding, the 100 laps lined up as scheduled.

Foyt is pissed off—of course—worse than anybody. Anthony Joseph Jr. is right on the verge. In 1961 A. J. has so far raced 35 times in nine states in seven months—roughly the equivalent of one midget, sprint, and champ car show per weekend—and he's won the Indy 500, bounced to victory around Langhorne's lethal lip, conquered DuQuoin and the Hoosier Hundred, and clinched the national big car title for the second consecutive year. In addition, he and an underdog 220 Offy have spent the summer getting it on with the short-stroke Chevys of Parnelli Jones and Jim Hurtubise in a dazzling series of sprint car fire fights. So with 18 first places in major and minor shows already, what could be left for A. J. to win? Merely the unofficial but priceless mantle of "greatest living dirt track driver." Vacant since the combat deaths of Bryan and

Eddie Sachs, champion of the shock-filled 1956 Atlanta 100. *Bob Tronolone*

Bettenhausen, the tag is all A. J.'s, providing he cap 1961 doing something especially brilliant.

The Action Track provides the big opportunity. Because he's already won Turkey Night the previous season, A. J., prior to missing the show, had automatically imagined that the Hut Hundred belonged to him too. And he still does. Desperate to torture some iron, he leads a coalition of his sugar-daddy friends into the camp of Terre Haute's 35th fastest qualifier, Don Northan. The dialogue is brief. What kind of booty would it take to make Northan, an underfinanced journeyman, abandon his dead-last starting post and surrender it to Foyt?

Northan contemplates the vastest sum imaginable—200 bones. "O.K.," A. J. agrees. "I got 100 of it myself, here." His sugar daddies kick in the rest. Don

Northam couldn't know it, but in addition to the fast $200, he is about to earn himself an asterisk in the chronicles of dirt racing.

The 100 ragged laps commence on a track where passing is impossible. But Foyt and his screaming mount, the *Hank Green Offy*, hunt down everything, and everyone. Thirty-fifth to 29th in a lap. Twenty-ninth to 10th in 10. Tenth to sixth in 15.

He is beating all the breath out of the rest of the field. Breaking its underbelly, Jim Hurtubise's midget digs into the goo, and the wild-eyed one almost gets upended by his own car. And then Bobby Wente, running first, quits with a mud-packed cockpit.

A. J. is the Hut Hundred's new leader. Yet if he doesn't climb off the choppy inside hardtack and discover a new groove, Foyt's *Hank Green* rig, too, will die. So A. J. develops ideas about taking it upstairs, to Terre Haute's outermost lane. Lap after lap he grabs tentative bites out of the slop. Then he irons everything semismooth, jumps on top of it and starts dancing, and now it really is all over.

Officials call off the afternoon nightmare show at 75 laps. Fading light, they alibi. Or maybe because Foyt had by then racked enough misery on the pulverized field, having lapped fifth place twice, doubled sixth place three times, and seventh place four.

Bettenhausen and Bryan are truly gone, so long live the new living sovereign of dirt—king A. J. The only problem is that not enough people have been at Terre Haute to witness the coronation, maybe only a few thousand. The foul conditions chased everybody else home early.

Bogie

Some 230 miles south of Los Angeles, almost in sight of the Cal/Mex frontier, I'm deep in the Cochella Valley attending yet another powerful addition of the venerable Mid-Winter Fair and the Saturday-Sunday sprint car program of the California Racing Association at the Imperial Valley Fairgrounds. It's 1963 and Imperial already has so much history it can give you indigestion.

A lot of it is somewhat unsavory, but if you take away all the unsavory bits, dirt racing might not have much history at all. Imperial's troubles began far back in 1934 with the Ernie Triplett/Al Gordon bloodbath; followed by the ghastly Forrest Lawn funeral where the widow Triplett was harassed by the hit-and-run lensmen and yellow scribblers of William Randolph Hearst; followed by the retaliation "kidnappings" of some of the Hearst photogs. And this was followed by William Randolph and his waves of attack hacks and sob sisters year after year going all out to persecute and abolish racing with their sensational headlines, apocalyptic prophesies, and the terrifying antiracing rallying cry, "A vigorous campaign against legalized murder!"

Wherever you look, Imperial's history has something strange and unlikely to offer. "Upside-Down" Jack Rounds got off to a ripping start in 1958 by flying off turn one and clobbering the oleander foliage on Saturday, then returning to crash-land the *Pop Miller Chevy* atop a parked ambulance on Sunday. Another Imperial sport named Ron "Full-Race" Cummings succeeded in losing control of a silly tub he'd purchased from Jim Hurtubise and splintered a timber fence, taking a

Them there eyes! Jim Hurtubise's dazzling headlamps may not have made his life easier, but they seemed to let him see things the rest of us couldn't. Dirt racing was never the same after Herk's surprise arrival. *Bob Tronolone*

27

A photo to savor. Herk wins the Sac 100 on October 25, 1959. *Bob Tronolone*

plank square in the guts. It was a big plank, too, and, as Imperial lore has it, before Full-Race could be fit inside the meatmobile—maybe it was the same one that Upside-Down hit—carpenters first had to saw it in two. Watching the sawing grossed out one and all, including even the young Parnelli Jones, but Full-Race lived and prospered and raced again. Yet another time, Rosie Roussel simultaneously wadded a careening sprinter and brought down Imperial's old timing platform with the timers standing on it; again, no major trauma ensued.

So at this installment of the Mid-Winter Fair I'm standing between turns one and two watching and listening to the stroker V-8s of the CRA in total contentment. The main event is only three laps down, but already checking out is "Lover Boy" Bobby Hogle, the CRA's marque driver, and his rare Offy-powered *Tamale Wagon*—race cars also have nicknames in

Southern California. Abruptly, though, I observe a black bogey coming up from the back and engaging the pack as it sweeps out of my sight onto the front straightaway. By the time everyone pops back into view, the black bogey is leading. It's an Elmer George car with a great pedigree and it wins by hours.

In the winners circle, out of the bogey's wheelhouse springs its pilot, a Tommy Hinnershitz–type farmer-looking guy—Gordon Wooley. Gordon's placid face belies the fact that he's a hired pistolero from Waco, Texas, with membership in sprinter associations all over the country. Also appearing is Don Shepherd, the black bogey's custodian, mechanic, and baby brother of out-of-the-ballpark A. J. Shepherd. Don, called "Shep," is a racing buccaneer—if he were to fly a racing flag of convenience, it would be the Jolly Roger. Shep's one of the last of the sprint car pirates, and he and his hired-gun chauffeurs ride the circuit everywhere from Pennsylvania

to California, raiding all the territories—USAC, IMCA, now the CRA—in search of booty and glory and easy pickin's. Just to get to Imperial, Shep hopscotched clear across the continent from an IMCA meet at Tampa, where he'd fired his assigned driver to shanghai Wooley.

The CRA boys go to bed Saturday night humiliated. But Sunday morning they sense trouble again when they find Shep on the starting line grinning at them like an ax murderer. The bastard is getting ready to do it to us again!

This time it won't be so easy. Not a drop of water gets dumped on Imperial's top lane, so Gordon Wooley's groove of the previous day is gone. Throughout qualifying heats CRA cars are on patrol, sweeping the track ahead of them clean and keeping Gordon behind. Even when Gordon starts the main event from the front row, an Arizonan named Gene "Tiger" Brown in a fast CRA car beats him into the corner.

Gordon sits behind, waiting Tiger out. Then there's another universe heard from. Coming on a kamikaze mission from ninth to third in four laps is Lover Boy Hogle and the *Tamale Wagon*. This impending meeting between Lover Boy, Gordon, and Shep promises to be interesting in the extreme. Lover Boy and Shep, it turns out, are well acquainted. Making a rare out-of-California start, Lover Boy had been Shep's assigned driver at Tampa. But Shep can't tolerate token race drivers, and after Lover Boy raced like he'd telephoned in his performance, Shep had hired Gordon and then bounced Lover Boy when he got to him.

Lover Boy took his Tampa firing personally and at Imperial is out to show Shep. But vendetta clouds Lover Boy's judgment. Trying to go three abreast with Tiger Brown and Gordon, where there's no room, Lover Boy and the *Tamale Wagon* evacuate Imperial in a hurry. Landing on his wheels, Lover Boy is mostly

Toy-sized midgets had all the good dirt stuff like speed, torque, and muscle beneath the hood. They just didn't have it in the same quantities as sprint and champ cars, but if you raced well in a midget, odds were you'd one day graduate to the bigger hogs. *Charley Fritz, Scalzo collection*

unhurt. His only pain is observing Gordon overcoming Tiger and watching Shep win again.

Pausing just long enough to collect first-place cash, Shep packs up and bats away, wheeling eastward to Illinois and a jerkwater IMCA affair where he satisfies a long-standing desire and defeats a legendary Hectore Honore sprinter on its home turf. Then he hauls farther east for some real-steel jousting at Langhorne.

Machine-Gunned

It's still 1963, and I'm at the Illinois State Fairgrounds, out on the Abraham Lincoln prairie, perched just outside of turn four and standing all by myself on the roof of the flimsiest wooden scoring shack you ever saw. This is the pace lap of the Springfield 100, and the first three rows are throttling past: the pearl, red, and blue *Sheraton-Thompson Special No. 2* flanked by the candy apple red *J. H. Rose 46*; the blue and red *Econo Rental 5* next to the white, red, and blue *Leader Card 1*; and the white and blue *Leader Card 4* alongside the pearl, blue, and red *Agajanian 98*. Or, to put it driver for

driver: A. J. Foyt/Johnny Rutherford; Bobby Marshman/Rodger Ward; Don Branson/Parnelli Jones. They're so close, I can smell the alky of the Offenhausers.

By now I'm well on my way to acquiring a solid dirt track writer's education. Making my bones, as it were, at Ascot Park I once had a hard clod of soil off Herk Hurtubise's right rear club my forehead and draw blood; at that same Ascot, while a main event was in progress, I dodged sprint cars in total darkness after a transformer blew out and took down all the stadium lights. On a deathtrap charter flight hosted by the Agajanian 98 Fan Club, I flew to the Sacramento mile aboard a wheezing old banger so clapped out it may have still been carrying camouflage left over from the Bay of Pigs. At the Phoenix mile, to get a better panorama, I broke all rules and crept into a Do Not Enter area to hide crouching on a barn top while hard-faced cowboy rent-a-cops directly below patrolled on full alert with giant grinning police dogs. . . .

But this Springfield adventure-in-progress is my most precarious yet. So that I may better understand

and even feel the muscle and heat of dirt champ cars, I'm stationed on this deserted scoring shack almost within touching distance of the beasts.

Where I am may well turn out to be the crossroads of hell, but it's too late to leave. Right in front of me is where Pat Flaherty crashed in 1956, and up the race track a ways is where Rex Easton did in 1961. It's impossible for me to know it now, but Billy Horstmeyer will experience terminal trouble here in 1964, and fearless Herk—perhaps Springfield's fastest flier until getting burnt and broken up on pavement—will sail over the top of this place in 1968 and go splat against some parked grading tractors. And still race at Milwaukee the following afternoon.

I wish it were 1952. That was the Illinois State Fair when Bill Schindler, the phenomenal pegleg, got loose on Springfield and really set a record. A pre–World War II luminary who founded the American Racing Drivers Club, the ARDC, Bill the Bronco originally trained in midgets up and down the East Coast, mastering their buzzing, breakaway moves to the tune of 53 feature wins for two seasons straight. Accustomed to flat and banked joints a quarter of a mile and tinier, Schindler was no less at home on the long miles: he won Springfield's 1952 100 with a speed average that exceeded Langhorne's standing world record.

Amazing as it sounds, Bronco hadn't even been Springfield's fastest driver. Far quicker was Troy Ruttman, the Jimmy Bryan–sized prodigy with the natural gift for dirt tracking similar to Troy's own L.A. forebear Frank Lockhart.

Barely 22, big Troy in 1952 was all ready to be appointed the globe's top wheelman on dirt—and perhaps pavement, too. Growing up in an L.A. colony of dust bowl émigrés, Rutt, exactly like a member of the Joad clan in *The Grapes of Wrath,* had a way with cars. At 16, he'd run the family heap to the local Ashcan Derby and won. Within a year, he was the boy wonder of the L.A. scene; racing hot rod track roadsters and midgets six nights a week, he was restless and impossible to be around every empty seventh day.

There was no other dirt shrine on the West Coast quite like it, and perhaps that was a blessing. This is the Imperial Fairgrounds. *Dwight Vaccaro*

He took his act nationally: setting records at Langhorne, winning on the do-or-die slant tracks of Salem, Winchester, and Dayton, and employing a used Merc to beat up on Ferraris in the Mexican road race; a dirt track Kuzma to outlast Vookie's *Fuel Injection Special* roadster in the Indy 500; a borrowed rail job to beat Tommy Hinnershitz over east, and a bathtub Hornet of his own to blow off Hudson icon Marshall Teague.

By the summer of 1952, then, just about the last thing Troy hadn't yet done was conquer a mile. Hence, he was only "almost" racing's top gun. But on that searing Springfield afternoon he was long gone—he'd already put Schindler, Mike Nazaruk, and everybody a lap behind—when he toasted the tires, had to pit for new rubber, and lost. Later the same week, Troy had the steering of his *98 Jr.* sprint car come apart at Hawkeye Downs in Cedar Rapids, and after the ensuing crash,

was never quite the same again. The bad luck found other drivers, too. A couple of weeks later, Bill Schindler took a stretched midget to Allentown and was killed in an off-track smash on the same afternoon that Frank Luptow of "Black Panther" Offy renown met the same fate in a stocker down South.

But it isn't 1952 anymore. It's 11 years later and Springfield 1963 is looking good. There's a 14-inch surface such as A. J., Johnny, Bobby, Rodger, Don, and Parnelli love getting sideways in. The field of 18 is massing right in front of me. Green flag!

Anticipating the obliterating torque of the *J. H. Rose* bow-tie V-8 of Johnny Rutherford, A. J. Foyt hangs Johnny out to dry on the top, and all eight outside cars behind Johnny are also momentarily trapped. Don Branson sees his big chance. From third row inside he veers low, grabs first, and here comes the whole pack highballing off of four with everybody aiming straight at me atop the shack!

Branson explodes past—CRASHBOOM!—followed by 17 other CRASHBOOMS! followed by a dark mass of Springfield agriculture that has me diving for cover because I'm getting machine-gunned. The damn stuff stings! The air clears somewhat and I feel free to glance up, but here come Branson and company already completing the lap and preparing to pot me all over again.

It's target practice! The fusillade threatens to blow me right off the pathetic roof, so for 10 laps I'm prostrated flat on my belly and hanging on; eyes wide shut, I don't even watch the race, just listen to the CRASH-BOOMS! And when the loose surface at last blows away and I can look up, everything has changed.

Branson's *Leader Card 4* isn't yet rigged out with power steering, so poor Don has fatigued and faded. Newly in the lead is Bobby Marshman, but here comes Foyt. I wait for A. J. to take over the race but it doesn't happen because Foyt, too, is apparently in some form

The *Tamale Wagon* Offy raced so furiously by Lover Boy Hogle at the 1963 Imperial belonged to the clan Morales, a racing family of seven brothers, plus various nephews and cousins, active in L.A. racing since Legion Ascot in the 1930s.
Scalzo collection

of distress, as is Parnelli Jones, and as is Johnny Rutherford, whose ailing V-8 has alcohol gargling out its injector stacks. Leader Marshman, too, will soon be dead meat, because in the final furlongs Rodger Ward arrives from nowhere to put the screws to him. Rodger is mile-trackdom's poised and ever canny vet who has the mind of an elephant when it comes to remembering and taking advantage of his opponents' moves and mistakes. Once again Rodger has let everybody do themselves in one by one, and has won the third Springfield of his career.

My body is bruised black and blue from top to bottom, and the only education I pick up at Springfield is to never again find myself on the outside of a heavy race track filled with dirt champ cars. Well, duh!

Night

By day Ascot Park in 1964 consists of a grim stand of vacant blue-gray parking lots, a confusion of tumbledown bleachers supported by a base of submerged junker hulks, and a hell's half-mile oval spread over the top of an abandoned landfill.

Dirt track racing, a uniquely American invention, like jazz—and, just like jazz, complete with wild tempo changes and mad improvisations and madder characters—was never the fastest or most efficient way of traveling 15 miles in a midget or sprinter, or 100 miles in a dirt champ car. It wasn't supposed to be. A track surface could dig up and pound the cars. There could be blinding dust. Somebody could run into somebody else and bring out the yellow. The stewards running the show, whether they were from 3-A or USAC, could blunder and make a controversy. Anxiety and uncertainty were part of the dirt mystique. *Bob Tronolone*

Brilliant but snake-bit, Troy Ruttman had the most frustrated and frustrating career of the 1951–1971 epoch. His admirers insisted that the likes of Bettenhausen, Bryan, and Foyt could not have won their various championships had Troy behaved better and been at full strength. *Scalzo collection*

Just to make matters ultracozy, the whole woebegone scene is parked near the Pacific harbor bottom of L.A., hard by the seedy gambling lairs and cheap booze dives of nowheresville Gardena.

Yet here's the same Ascot on a foggy cold sprint car Saturday night with all stadium lights ablaze and the injected Chevys pounding your skull in tempo with the cackling and boiling Offys: fantasyland, a kind of paradise on earth.

The fan dance of nighttime dirt track racing! What is there about nighttime combat that makes everything

rev up so much harder than by dull day? Danger and adrenaline and endorphins are foxtrotting everywhere. And many of the great moments of my life happen during full-moon Saturdays when the homegrown heroes of the CRA are out there doing the Ascot back-it-in.

But Ascot this special evening is hosting the sterling personalities and succulent equipment of USAC. USAC sprint car racing is suddenly the wildest contest going anywhere, maybe the most supercharged dirt track racing there's ever been. "Driving like a USAC sprint car driver" means taking a flying leap at a pack of sprinters and jamming for a crucial extra foot in the very first corner, then blunting your nerve endings and not cooling the tempo till the checkered flag waves over the dust.

Combatants are Indy 500 luminosities like A. J., Parnelli, and Herk; or else they're young 500 wannabes such as Johnny Rutherford, Mario Andretti, and Bobby Unser. This Ascot night belongs to Bobby. Leading all the way from the outside front row, he first holds off A. J., then beats his old mentor Parnelli, and gets his very first USAC feature. And Bobby accomplishes it racing the iron of our old Imperial friend, freebooter Don Shepherd.

These USAC folks are one big family, eager minds all in one place, and after racing really know how to lay on a party and do the sauce, chick, and troubadour number till dawn and beyond. So, whenever they're out at Ascot, ground central is the Motel Dorrick, where the lobby parties are enormous: racers, girls, firecrackers, intoxicants, laughter. Things can get crazy, but normally you won't get busted for disorderly conduct, not even the evening when Roger McCluskey was in hot pursuit of Johnny White with a steak knife as payback for some earlier Johnny shenanigans.

This particular evening at the Dorrick will ease into insider legend courtesy of a guerrilla mechanic and special pard of Bobby Unser's named Howard "Tilt" Millican. Early accounts of Tilt center on a sublime moment in Pecos, Texas. Visiting a cowpoke saloon there, he'd headed straight for the cowgirls' table. Some of the cowpokes took offense and proceeded to carry Tilt out into the street and beat the crap out of him. So Tilt was forced to settle accounts by scaling the fence of a National Guard armory, starting up and pilfering an army tank, then using it to fight his way back inside the saloon by collapsing the front door.

Tilt's expressive face is as furrowed as the Phoenix mile; serious wear and tear is one price of being a wild man deluxe. On this Dorrick night, for reasons that don't need going into, Tilt gets locked inside a third-floor motel room. Not wanting to miss the lobby highjinks, he escapes by going over the landing and free-falling onto an open balcony. Discovering a balcony door ajar, he wanders into the adjoining darkened bedroom. When a screaming female jackknifes straight up in bed demanding to know who he is, Tilt, who of course means her no harm, explains that he's leaving and for her to go back to sleep. But his soothing words don't allay the woman's fears and she screams harder.

Two greats exchanging "how ya doin's?"—Troy Ruttman, in car, and Tommy Hinnershitz, Sacramento 1958.
Bob Tronolone

Waking up in the emergency ward of a crash house with his bell ringing and IV tubes poking into his arms was often the fate of even a top dirt tracker. But it wasn't the sort of career move that interested Rodger Ward, whose racing aim was to achieve longevity by not getting hurt. Rodger did the best job of winning throughout the 1950s and 1960s and escaping in one piece. *Bob Tronolone*

To picture Tilt properly, you have to know the source of his name. During boyhood, a runaway Harley-Davidson—followed by a case of polio—did unspeakable things to his pelvis. He emerged from rehab with one leg significantly shorter than the other, so he became "Tilt."

The fuzz confront our tilted balcony-jumper in a stairwell. And Tilt now has to haul ass galloping sideways as only he can. He leads the heat down a couple flights of stairs, then across the lobby and straight through the middle of the sprint car party where everything's running wide open. Drivers, car owners, mechanics, hangers-on, and perhaps one or two disrobed damsels all disappear, dashing into the gritty Gardena night. In the confusion, Tilt gets away, lying low in the motel kitchen . . .

The Last Rim Ride

It's 1966, and I'm back at the Mid-Winter Fair at Imperial—I can't stay away! And as Sunday's main event cars line up, the dirt track paparazzi are incredulously but joyfully checking out the rubber combination of a California Racing Association sprinter raced by Dick Fries. Dick's got lofty ambitions. His double-step knobs tell us he's deadly serious and preparing to go for it: come the drop of the green, he'll be planting his rump up on the top lane where he'll fire off skyrockets of earth rim-riding Imperial.

Once dirt racing's hottest spectating treat, rim-riding of late has deteriorated into almost a dead art.

Nobody is certain why. Some claim that the beginning of the end was when Parnelli Jones and Jim Hurtubise used their stock-block dreadnoughts to run the high-strung 220-cube Offenhausers out of the dirt track game. Offy four-bangers had short and nervous power bands; they had to be wound up and buzzed. By contrast, bent-eight Chevys hooked up, pounded, and ate dirt tracks alive. But others insist that, no, the bigger and wider tires of the 1960s are responsible for making track surfaces go hard and slick.

Still, even though it's open to debate, rim-riding probably used to be choicest in the IMCA, where the likes of A. J. Shepherd and Leroy Neumayer and their yellow and orange *Diz Wilson Nos. 70* and *71* were werewolves carrying on with throttle and steering wheels and living in every top lane of the cornstalk circuit; and naturally over in eastern P-A where Tommy Hinnershitz held the franchise for raising pulses. Unfortunately for people not living over east,

Tommy was a homeboy who seldom brought his act west of the Appalachians. One day in 1963, though, a Pennsy neighbor and would-be emulator of Tommy's did come out to Terre Haute and mounted a rim-riding conquest of the Action Track. He was Bobby Marshman.

Making ready to rumble, the Action Track's pack of sprinters appeared to be much like a booming big band of hepcat jazz musicians all impatient to improvise and blow at blinding tempo. And, who could tell? Perhaps the most far-out solo was going to be authored by the ensemble's most innocuous-looking member.

At Terre Haute that was Marshman, the gentle-natured, long-necked son of a racing promoter. Stuck back in the seventh hole, Bobby was on the pedal of the *Econo Car 7*, one of Eddie Kuzma's few sprint cars, owned and prepped by Wally Meskowski.

Why so stern-looking, Tilt? Howard "Tilt" Millican was one wild man deluxe, and a perfect fit for the whole roaring atmosphere of friendship, laughs, chicks, fights, and the vivid threat of annihilation that surrounded mid-1960s USAC sprint car racing. Tilt once hijacked an army tank and smashed it through a bar front, took off and crash-landed a helicopter without instruction or a license, and was prone to setting a match to a mouthful of cigarette lighter fluid and snorting fire. He was also a hot dog guerrilla mechanic who could take almost any sprinter and make it run faster—and not a bad race driver himself. *Bob Tronolone*

Drivers meeting for some of the USAC wonder kids circa 1965. *Bob Tronolone*

Go! Boldly jumping right on top of the cushion, Bobby tried going rim-riding immediately. Everybody else played it safe and dull down on Terre Haute's wind-blazed bottom and middle lanes.

Live by the rim-rider sword, or die by it. Bobby at first looked like he was all done. The only rim-rider there, he was flailing and fighting the wheel, trying to sweep Terre Haute's cush' clean all by himself. The timid suckers down on the middle and bottom were freight-training his can.

But on lap seven he moved to fifth. On lap eight he was fourth. The rim was heating up, a holy tension was building, and Bobby was making Terre Haute begin to

swing. Four laps later he and *No. 7* grabbed third. The rim was the place to be! Continuing the wild count-down, Bobby on lap 15 caught Don Branson for sec-ond. On lap 25 he blew past Roger McCluskey for first.

Bobby had achieved full momentum and became a hot-soloing hornman: given the opportunity to stand up and blow tenor like Zoot Sims, he would only quit when nothing was left.

"Look at me, the only bad-guy rim-rider!" he seemed to say. "The rest of you goody-two-shoes don't have what it takes to rim-ride!"

And indeed that day they hadn't, except when it was too late. By the checkered, McCluskey, Branson,

and everybody else was up on the rim following and aping Bobby, looking for a chance to play front-runner that never came.

Here at Imperial, brave Dick Fries is about to try a "Bobby Marshman" and Allah praise him for that. A real blast from the past. For whatever it's worth, Dick's no gentle creature like the late Bobby, and in future decades will mature into a drug thug: he and a desperado pal, who for awhile tooled the country's only sprint car with a Jimmy supercharger, will draw two-year vacations in the slammer for hawking loco weed by air and on the high seas.

Right now, though, Dick's ready to throw on some hot rim-riding entertainment. Imperial lacks outside guardrails, so should Dick require an emergency exit while in the middle of his rim-ride he can always jump the corners at the risk of taking down a stand of small trees.

Alas, on the afternoon of what may have been dirt racing's last epic rim-ride, Imperial's rim quickly goes away. There's no traction upstairs. So, following several dramatic but futile laps and untold wasted heartbeats, Dick has to drop back downstairs with all the mere mortals. He can't make up the lost ground and finishes at the caboose.

Flower Child

It's 1969, the two unequaled decades are nearing an end, and classic dirt track racing is going out of fashion

Rim-riding—moving out of the regular racing groove seeking greater momentum patrolling in the jagged dirt piled up on the track rim—was generous racing. It revved up your pulse, bulged your eyes, and afterward left you with an indelible memory to take home after the race. Bobby Marshman, this time in the *Hopins 5* Meskowski, shows how it was done. *George Johnstone, Scalzo collection*

There can never be too many pictures of Don Branson. Or of Jud Larson. Here the pair of masters are together at 1964's Sacramento 100, Jud low for a change, Don up high. *Dan Mahony*

not with a roar but a sob as the wise men of USAC indifferently contemplate stripping dirt tracks from the national championship calendar. The bull market is over, and dirt track personalities themselves have already been disenfranchised to pariah status at the reinvented Indianapolis—even "Son-of-Panzer" Gary Bettenhausen will have a hard time finding an Indy ride, because the 500 has turned aggressively commercial, foreign, and pompous.

The dirt track tramps from the hinterlands do what comes naturally: they rebel. Jeering at what they consider the fake glitz and decadence of Indy, they've adopted their own mocking outlaw dishabille—kind of like Jud Larson at the 1956 Hoosier Hundred!—and dress down in weather-beaten jeans, grimy racing T-shirts, and grubby track shoes. All are racing at tonight's Iowa extravaganza in Knoxville on the Marion County Fairgrounds' banked half-mile of gleaming black gumbo.

Following three furious nights of time trials, heats, last-chance consolations, and other sudden-death eliminations, the "Knoxville Nationals" is about to send a bulky pack of 24 sprinters plunging into turn one for 15 searing miles in hot pursuit of the big bucks.

Here at Knoxville, sprint cars have their bays overfilled with no-limit V-8s and wear clodhopper rubber on all four corners—their bulky contours repudiate and disparage the natural lines of the aesthetic and artsy-craftsy Watsons, Phillips, and Meskowskis of just a few campaigns ago.

And unlike Bobby Unser, Johnny Rutherford, and Mario Andretti—who competed minus kick-off and nerf-bar armor and who usually disdained physical contact and going on their nobs—the latest tramp drivers are bump-and-gouge merchants who don't object to getting violently upside down. Giving them more courage to do so are the protective rollover cockpit cages that came on the scene following the 1966 wrenching deaths of the uncanny Larson and the unequaled antique Don Branson. Iron roll cages may well be the visual ruin of sprint, midget, and dirt champ cars, but at long last a driver's first line of defense isn't his own skull, neck, and shoulders when his open-cockpit tumbles. And tumble these roll-cage tramps do!

Knoxville's champion this night will be Kenny Gritz, product of the short-tracks of Nebraska, whose face in the winners circle is all wrecked and bearing burn marks from an acetylene torch mishap. Kenny's not headed for stardom, but martyrdom. Just a couple of weeks from now he'll be ordered to remove his roll cage at an open-cockpit meet and get the chop when he overturns.

But posterity demands that Jan Opperman—Knoxville runner-up to Kenny—get his due because Jan is the electric freak presence who is dirt tracking's future.

Opp was imported to the Knoxville straight out of a California long-hair commune. An Age-of-Aquarius devotee brimming over with counterculture dogma, he spent Thursday and Friday sharing grass, girls, and speed secrets with one and all, just like a good flower child must. But by Saturday, tonight, Opp-the-hippie is damaged goods with so miserable a head cold he can scarcely breathe. He's still running first in the Nationals with three laps to go until rendered blind and breathless after his goggles and face mask clog with mucus.

Bob Tronolone

"Son-of-Panzer" Gary Bettenhausen runs up on Bob Harkey. *Bob Tronolone*

By the mid-1960s all the raging short-stroke V-8s had run Offenhauser out of sprint car racing, and by 1969 the old Meyer-Drake four-cylinder had pretty much gotten the bum's rush from mile-track champ car competition as well. The front row of Sacramento has Greg Weld's Plymouth parked on pole. *Bob Tronolone*

During numerous pre–dirt track racing lifetimes, Opp did everything imaginable, so long as it was cool and full of humanity. Whatever works, he goes for! In the near future, he'll be reborn as a radical Christian minister. He'll also continue dirt track racing—like nobody's quite seen before. He'll organize his own attack-and-go outcast sprint car team and it will turn into a totally disorganized yet overachieving gang who at a moment's notice can rocket to any major or podunk race in the United States and win.

In addition to possessing the manic energy to motivate, inspire, enlighten, and alter almost anyone with whom he comes in contact, Opp soon will be raising so high the danger level of sprint car racing that those in his entourage will at times turn their faces to avoid the anxiety of watching him. "Chickens," Opp will reproach.

Taking a sledgehammer to the old stop-and-go racing patterns of the 1950s and 1960s, Opp and his go-for-it-all tastes will set in motion and win a 1970s sprint car and dirt track revolution whose traditions are with

us today. Whether Opp really intends it to happen quite that way is debatable, but suddenly everything revs up: after decades of unimportance, the gross weight of sprint, midget, and champ cars is deemed critical, and diet measures include the elimination of a race car's nose and grille, plus side and bottom panels. Tires big as barrels sprout; aluminum rat-motor V-8s of 410 cubes and 750 horses burst through hoods; plug-ugly air boxes and nose plates follow; and at last comes the coup de grace of race car uglification—over-the-cockpit "wings" as ungainly as garage doors.

All these new gizmos and bric-a-brac so traumatize and kill dirt tracks that after hot laps and long before the racing even begins, a typical track surface is already so rubber coated and smooth it might as well be pavement. But as the new millennium unfolds, the muscle-bound and follow-the-leader fare remains fantastically popular—who knows why?

And leading the way with all flags flying—until he gets blindsided and debilitated in 1976—will be Opp: the last charismatic dirt racer. From Panzer Tony to Opp the Flower Child in 20 years. Who'd have figured?

They're all going away and leaving us! The 1960 starting field at Sacramento rides away toward the horizon just as real dirt racing itself ultimately did. *Bob Tronolone*

Chapter 2

STAY OUT OF THE MARBLE ORCHARD

To Please a Lady, a tale of a heartless race driver versus a black widow spider reporter, is a 1950 flick starring Clark Gable and Barbara Stanwyck that may well be the tom turkey of all Hollywood howler racing movies. Yet the film nearly redeems itself with a single shouted word: "Indianapolis!" The shouter is Adolphe Menjou, a yes-man to Stanwyck, and with that word old Adolphe really nails it: he unexpectedly brings forth all of the rainbow's-end drama and emotion that Indy held for American race drivers of the 1951–1971 vintage. Really winding himself up and making an aria, Menjou explodes, "INN-DEE-AN-APP-POH-LUS!!"

Whether you were a raw-but-expectant rookie or some cynical hack, Indy truly was INN-DEE-AN-APP-POH-LUS: the 500 was the reason why you raced. It was your ultimate goal and target. And not merely for all that Brickyard glory and mazuma, either, but also because in the minds of right-thinking racing people you just weren't much until you were among the select 33 taking the green flag on Memorial Day.

Well and good. But, how, exactly, did one get to take part in the golden 500? Well, you'll be surprised to hear that from 1951–1971 the path was fairly simple. Say you were some aspiring hotshot with lead in your toes and an overheated brain obsessed with Indy: all you had to do was ride back to the Brickyard on a carpet of dirt.

It was really easy, and anybody could do it: start out young, poor, and a nobody, load up on the dirt track train, then finish up a hero of the 500. And the world of dirt racing actually offered greater rewards than that. Perhaps there'd come a time in an Indy winner's life—after he was rich, decadent, and disillusioned—when he'd take pleasure in realizing that his best moves, memories, and friendships hadn't been formed on the dull Brickyard at all, but back when he and his running buddies were mad dreamers strapping on midgets, sprinters, and big champ cars to prep for Indy on the wild dirt of Springfield, Reading, and Terre Haute.

Unhappily, though, there were not one but two possible final destinations for the dirt track warrior. One was the Indy 500, where everybody wanted to go; the second was where *nobody* wanted to go.

The sanctimonious called it "the golden speedway." But the racers were less flowery; it was just the way they talked. "The marble orchard," was their term.

Parnelli, Herk, and A. J.

The 35th Indy 500, held in 1951, was the beginning of the 20-year-long dirt explosion and a barometer of all to come. Peppering the field were bravos fresh off the sod highway, mostly from California and many from Los Angeles; they were popping the 500 wide open. Among them were: Walt Faulkner, the Gilmore

Herk's big Sacramento mile-track day of October 25, 1959. Starting 11th, he had the lead by the halfway point, ultimately winning by a lap. *Bob Tronolone*

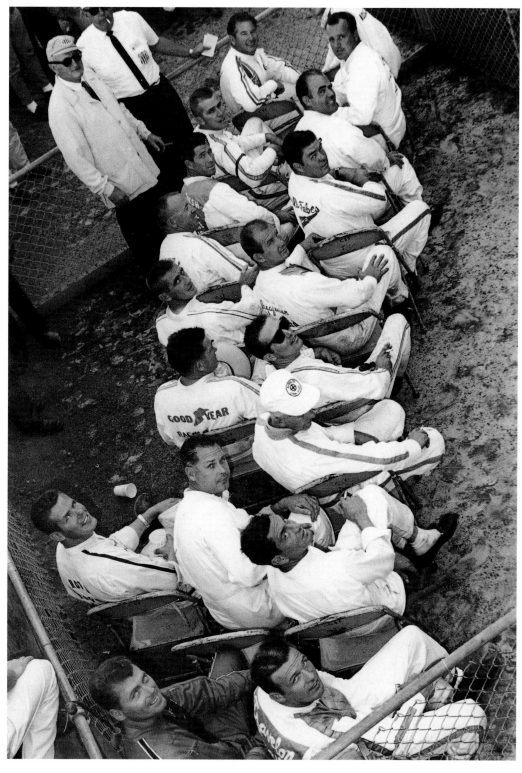

Starting field of the 1963 Sacramento 100: Rodger Ward and Johnny Rutherford; Bobby Marshman and A. J. Foyt; Roger McCluskey and Chuck Hulse; Don Branson and Jimmy McElreath; Johnny White and Parnelli Jones; Jim Hurtubise and Bud Tinglestad; Lloyd Ruby and Bobby Unser; Billy Cantrell and Bobby Grim; Bob Harkey and Chuck Booth. *Dan Mahony*

Stadium midgeteer who originally came to the Brickyard the year before with Clay Smith, and who at three seconds before the 6 P.M. track closing broke the old Ralph Hepburn Novi speed records by two miles per hour, now in 1951 with a prototype Kuzma smashed them by four, 15th place; Jack McGrath, "the nitro man" from hot rodding who for five successive years would sit on Indy front rows with speed records of his own, 3rd; Andy Linden, the tattooed rookie, 4th; Bobby Ball and Joie James, also vintage rookies, 5th and 33rd, and both headed for the marble orchard; and, of course, the terrific trio with future dates to get their mugs carved into the Borg-Warner winner's trophy: the brilliant Okie Troy Ruttman, 23rd; the underrated Rodger Ward, 27th; and way back in 29th the national midget champion and American Nuvolari, Billy Vukovich.

As he did with almost everything—until getting wiped out by private traumas and a string of suspensions—Ruttman mastered the dirt highway fastest, winning Indy in 1952. Then in 1953 and 1954 it was the dominating Vukovich, especially in the heat-poisoned sweepstakes of 1953. Still, Vookie almost got upstaged by the dramatics of Andy Linden, who strutted the formidable stuff that dirt track troopers were made of.

Andy began his 500 with a third-lap crash and a fire that produced second-degree burns, a hysterical wife, and a cot in the infield crashhouse. Then he gained his freedom by promising the medics that if they let him go he wouldn't try rejoining the 500. Well, Asbestos Andy proceeded to violate that promise the first time by relieving heat-stricken Chuck Stevenson, and then he broke it a second time spelling a similarly wiped-out Rodger Ward. That one put Andy back into the hospital where physicians and nurses alike lined up for the privilege of ripping him a new one. But, as Andy remarked in his defense, he just couldn't let his L.A. buddies down.

To live in Los Angeles in the mid-1950s and be an aspiring dirt track highway traveler was like being in a candy store—Walt, Jack, Andy, Troy, Rodger, Vookie up in Fresno, and so many other overachievers to try to emulate. So which one of the stars did you pick as role model? Rufus Parnell Jones—who in time would be transformed into "Parnelli"—made his choice while he was a teenager standing outside Carrell Speedway and listening to somebody inside playing an Offy midget like a musical instrument. It was Troy Ruttman, and Parnelli decided on the spot that the truth was with big Rutt.

Troy had started out racing in a low-life series known as the "Ashcan Derby"; by Parnelli's time the same junker tournament had put on the ritz and become "Jalopy Derby," complete with TV broadcasts live from the Gardena Bowl: as many as 100 steel heaps showed up every Sunday afternoon with only 18 survivors getting flagged into the main event. Just as in Rutt's day, it was a bargain-basement race driving academy of hard-knocks teaching red-meat aggression and various other invaluable licks to players like Scotty Cain, who used to get into marathon punch-outs; Van Johnson, whose hard-flipping jalopy once pitched its furiously revving engine and then had it crash-land and go right on with its furious revving; and, especially, Parnelli, who was particularly intimidating racing on mud.

His god Rutt hadn't soloed with jalopies. Learning the dirt track trade, Troy had raced everything everywhere, and so Parnelli, too, turned laps with all the racing clubs of L.A.—CJA, URA, CRA,

NASCAR—equally at home in jalops, sprints, midgets, super-modifieds, even taxicabs.

By 1959 the dirt highway to Indy was beckoning. But the rub was that the road began elsewhere: although L.A. could fairly boast that it had almost all the fastest drivers, smartest race car builders, wisest mechanics, most colorful stooges, and so forth, those race tracks where a dirt newcomer such as Parnelli was expected to make his bones and serious reputation were on the other side of the Mississippi.

So that June, after winning 11 of 16 L.A. main events, eastward went Parnelli with the *Fike Plumbing Special*, a typical California-style sprinter mating a honking V-8 Chevy—injected, Isky roller camshaft, the works—to a cooking Hank Henry chassis. In the company of Herk Hurtubise, Upside-Down Rounds, and A. J. Shepherd, he had an active tour of the IMCA.

Back in the Midwest again the following summer, in 1960, Parnelli traveled across Indiana to a USAC

Jud Larson, here with Parnelli Jones, was that anomaly of a dirt track driver who wanted nothing to do with the Indy 500—not unless the Hoosiers tossed some dirt on top of their bricks. And traveling 500 miles in a race car seemed like an exhausting eternity as well. Participating in a couple of Indys, Jud didn't do squat in either one, except break up his pit crew. It happened while he was stopping for tires, fuel, and perhaps what laid-back Jud was imagining might be an opportunity to have a smoke, drink a beer, and take a nap. But the crew had his roadster renovated and ready to go again almost before its wheels had stopped. "No!" Jud screeched in protest. "I'm not ready to go yet!" *Bob Tronolone*

Seat-of-the-pants machismo wasn't enough in L.A.'s school-of-hard-knocks Jalopy Derby. The scenario frequently demanded that daring deeds carried out on the track continue in the pits afterward, but not with steering wheels. Scotty Cain, in white, was always in the middle of rumbles. *Scalzo collection*

melee for midgets at Kokomo. His reputation preceded him, and he was hyped as the new Californian with the Ruttman pedigree. From his actions at Kokomo, though, Parnelli with his hard-guy puss seemed more in the tradition of Andy Linden. Battling Andy used to gesticulate with his boxer fists to move stragglers out of his way, and one afternoon at a slant track had a champion Midwestern driver cringing and hiding in terror

inside the infield crapper because Andy was angry and preparing to do a Rocky Marciano number on him when he found him.

Jalopy Derby–style aggression was Parnelli's trademark—at Kokomo he ran over everyone. The Kokomo regulars were ready to attack in retaliation but didn't dare because Parnelli wasn't alone and had brought along some rough friends.

Parnelli Jones, right, takes aim at Scotty Cain ahead. Emulating his role model Troy Ruttman, Parnelli apprenticed in everything from stocks to jalops to midgets. *Scalzo collection*

Early, early Jim Hurtubise. *Edward M. Huebner, Jake Bozony collection*

Shortly afterward, at his first sprint car start at Terre Haute, he got fined 50 smacks for jumping the start. At another midget race a car owner for a rival driver bitched so heatedly that one of Parnelli's rough buds lunged for him. "You can't hit me," cried the owner, "I'm wearing glasses." The mechanic finessed the problem by pulling off the glasses and breaking them in two; Parnelli was made to pay for a new pair. Occasionally, Parnelli came into contact with an even bigger rockhead than himself. Getting into a great bust-up with Rex Easton, he sent Rex's car twirling off the track. Rex returned with a two-by-four and heaved it at Parnelli from the infield while Parnelli was still racing.

Around this time Parnelli was taken in hand by enigmatic Johnnie Pouelsen, ex-hot rod roadster shoe, Offy expert, whiz at setting up lowbelly laydown dinosaurs, and perhaps the wisest Parnelli authority going. More than merely acting as Parnelli's chief mechanic, Johnnie well understood Parnelli's hyper-competitive ways and came close to being Parnelli's coach and personal trainer. Once the two of them became Firestone's main test team at Indy, for example, Johnnie—following a long day spent busting Flint-stones on the empty Speedway—would enter Parnelli

in a dirt midget race so Parnelli could unleash all his pent-up aggression on the unfortunate field.

Johnnie was just in time. Others had been getting ahead of Parnelli on the dirt highway. By the end of 1961, Parnelli had indeed collected some national sprint car titles, he'd fought astounding battles with Herk Hurtubise and A. J. Foyt, plus he'd won a bloody Phoenix champ car match. But his chum Hurtubise had done even better, including winning Sacramento, almost cracking 150 miles per hour at the Brickyard, and conquering Langhorne. And Jim Packard, a relative of a North Carolina hooch runner, and the supposed black-sheep heir of the Packard car company, had had three unexpected big races at Springfield, DuQuoin, and Syracuse where he just "Drove right by 'em." The "'em" included Eddie Sachs, Johnny Thomson, Foyt, and even the intimidating Tony Bettenhausen, whom Jim not only had zapped but had the impertinence to tap in the tail. And of course Foyt, two years younger than Parnelli, had by 1961 already nabbed two national champ car titles plus Indy itself.

But Parnelli was focused. In his freshman 500 of 1961 he discovered a groove and technique that nobody else could duplicate—not Hurtubise, not Foyt—and through the next three Memorial Days Parnelli became Indy's top-dog chauffeur, even though he won the 500 just once. Appropriately, he won it for Ruttman's old car owner, J. C. Agajanian. The dirt highway had worked again.

Perhaps no dirt track combatant since Bettenhausen had been such a hard-on as Parnelli, and yet Parnelli had smarts and great survival instincts: almost nobody on the dirt track highway experienced less personal injury. It was a riddle. Was being a badass the way you beat the marble orchard?

• • •

"I quit," Parnelli supposedly said to himself at the 1959 North Dakota State Fair at Minot, right at the beginning of his kindergarten training in the IMCA. "I'm not a race driver," Parnelli continued. "Hurtubise is a race driver, not me. I'll never be able to do stuff he does."

Tight friends already, Parnelli and Herk had come tooling into Minot in the company of yet another barnstormer on the dirt track highway, A. J. Shepherd, who had a rattletrap Olds 88 whose torn headliner was the bank where Herk stored all his prize money.

Parnelli was accustomed to the dust-free tracks of L.A., not those of the IMCA. And he'd seen Herk do insane things back in L.A., but no stunt Herk ever

Compared to a traditional Offy sprint car, a roaring V-8 Chevy sprinter was overpowered and overpowering. Grappling one into submission took arms, elbows, and soul. Parnelli and Herk, outside and inside, show how it was done. *Harry Goode, Scalzo collection*

A. J. Foyt and the insanely fast 220 Offy-powered *Bowes Seal Fast* Watson sprinter. A. J. wasn't prepared to concede that the Chevys of Parnelli and Herk were faster. *Bob Tronolone*

pulled had messed with Parnelli's mind like Minot. Everything was total dust, visibility zero. But Herk disappeared into it hammer-down anyway, as if those neon eyes of his provided special vision. Upside-Down Rounds was there, too, and the fight for first was between the two of them. Then Upside-Down made another payment on his nickname, flying out of the fairgrounds and almost hitting a Ferris wheel. Herk won and Parnelli was runner-up and ready to quit racing.

Parnelli repudiated his decision immediately, yet when Herk was on his rampage Parnelli wasn't the only one thinking along those lines. And maybe thinking,

too, that this crazy guy was one serious candidate for the marble orchard.

Born in upstate New York, Herk had his early hardtop racing semi-interrupted by a stint in the coast guard at Tampa. So that he wouldn't lose his steering wheel touch, on weekends he'd go AWOL from his gunboat by jumping overboard and swimming across Boca Ciega Bay to race more hardtops at Speedway Park.

Then around 1956, deciding to tap into the California scene and charbroil his brains in the L.A. sun and smog, he rode a motorcycle out West and saw a California Racing Association sprint meet on the frontier of Mexico at Imperial, the worst track in the West. Legend

Johnnie Pouelsen, background, was the airplane-loving Los Angeles race driver-turned-chief mechanic who became the coach and inseparable force behind Parnelli. Long before the two hooked up, Johnnie had already accomplished a lot. He'd zoomed out of the ballpark and got Hank Higuchi's hot rod wedged fast among Imperial's trees. In addition, he made a split-torsion bar midget, said to have been the best handling of its time. Later he stretched and ballasted a Kurtis-Kraft, adding a bigger engine to produce a flyaway sprinter that Johnnie named "Rollerskate." He also made a lay-down Indy roadster praised by Quin Epperly. Johnnie ended up paying for his airplane fixation in September of 1967 when his Twin Commanche went into the ground outside a small airstrip near Indianapolis. *Bob Tronolone*

A. J. and Wally Meskowski. *Scalzo collection*

A dirt driver's career was spent sending bounding, bucking, crossed-up race cars into 100-mile-per-hour corners edged by walls of wood, cement, trees, buildings, and sometimes even humanity. And all the while squinting desperately for vision while hurtling through blanketing dust and flying sod that camouflaged holes, ridges, ruts, and other cars. This is Rodger Ward at the end of his dirt track career in 1964. He and A. J. spent seven years storing up grudges and resentments and showing racing fans terrific battles. *Bob Tronolone*

chassis all by himself, then put a gear in the mother and go (it was said that Herk had to do things his own way, even when they didn't make mechanical sense, in order to psyche himself up to race the way he did). Not long after winning Minot, he visited Hawkeye Downs, the big half-mile in Cedar Rapids, Iowa, infamous for Troy Ruttman's accident. Hitting the guardrail entering the back straight, he flipped out of the track and then banged himself up doing five endos along the same set of railroad tracks that had gotten Rutt.

Trouble ran off Herk's shoulders like water, of course, and as soon as the croakers released him he towed eight hours to Indianapolis to repair his wrecked car inside a vacant stall in Gasoline Alley. Hobbling about with bruised ribs, a twisted ankle, and his trademark darting eyes all purple and blue from the effects of the flip, he overheard some Offy roadsters getting it on during Firestone tests and went out to watch them. He was unimpressed. Just prior to departing Indy to rejoin Parnelli at the Minnesota State Fair and also setting off a 10-sprinter spill, Herk, laughing as ever, observed that the vets were driving the corners all wrong and that the next time he came to the Speedway he'd show everybody how to run the big 150-mile-per-hour lap they were always talking about.

says that he proceeded to slap together his own sprint car in two weeks. It was a GMC-powered sled, painted blue and gray, with steering on the left side; its engine was a vibrating fool with one iron cylinder head and one aluminum head, and its tail used two Caddy fins that snapped off during Herk's first rollover.

Hitting the IMCA for the first time in 1958, one year before he and Parnelli did it together, he left in his wake scared-to-death fans, smashed sprinters, and broken-hearted car owners, but nobody could say Herkie didn't stand on the gas—in everything. Dropping by Moline, Illinois, one hot August night, he set fast time at the Quad City quarter-mile in a V-8 stock-block, blew it up, then went looking for any other warhead available to torture. He came up with an old ill-handling thing with an ancient Ranger airplane engine; it was terrible, and just completely wore out Herkie. Only fourth with one lap to go, he still jumped on it and then rammed past the last of the race's three leaders on the final corner to win.

So in 1959 Herk was doing the IMCA tournament yet again, this time in company with Parnelli. Always his own mechanic, he insisted on doing his own cars: seat the car owner up in the grandstands, set up the

Damned if he didn't. After closing out 1959 with his bold champ car win at Sacramento, the braggart with the bright eyes snagged a rookie ride in the *Travelon Trailer* dinosaur for the 1960 500 and the entire Indy establishment was lined up to watch him do a belly flop. But, once again, it was like jazz. "I'm here to blow!" Herk seemed to say. "Stand back and hear me blow!"

His 10-mile time trial spree of only four minutes was talked of with the kind of reverence that road racing purists reserved for Fangio's nine minutes in eternity on the Nurburgring. No, it hadn't quite been the big one-five-oh that Herkie-bear had forecast—the official average was 149.056 miles per hour—but it was a fat 3 miles per hour faster than anyone had ever gone before. And the 149.601 figure clocked by Herk on the third of his four rippers was a white-knuckler only .016 second shy of being Indy's first subminute lap.

Rodger Ward and the *Leader Card* Watson that in 1959 won DuQuoin and the Hoosier Hundred, plus USAC's national points championship. *Bob Tronolone*

Jack McGrath. The popular "Nitro Man," with his werewolf teeth, lost to the marble orchard on the Phoenix mile. *Russ Reed, Scalzo collection*

No dirt track combatant had ever cracked Indy with greater drama; and, having got his initial bang there, Herk kept going back for six consecutive 500s. But he could never get hooked up in the 500 the same way he did qualifying. Still, he continued riding 1960's momentum and glory.

At his bellwether best with USAC during 1960, 1961, and 1962, he won 18 dirt sprinters plus three 100-mile champ car shows. Every one was unforgettable in some way, especially Langhorne in June of 1960, where the great but aging Jimmy Bryan, who in his younger years had lorded it over "the big left turn," tore into Puke Hollow leading. But big Jimbo was unaware of the conspiracy of Don Branson, Upside-Down Rounds, Jim Packard, and Herkie that was forming just behind. Then somehow Bryan's car started going over, and the marble orchard had a new gravestone when the flips ended.

The race went on anyway. Branson, Rounds, and Packard—competitors Herk considered formidable—proceeded to run away for the first 30 miles. But then Herk caught the Langhorne fever and started coming on like a madman; putting all of his foes away, he began pulling clear. Packard, who was in amazing form, made a strong run for the flag, but Herkie still won.

And after earlier having paid Parnelli the enormous compliment of plagiarizing the *Fike Plumbing Special* and building a pounding Chevy sprinter of his own, Herk made himself master of Terre Haute. A. J. Foyt attended all the Action Track meets too, and wasn't prepared to concede that Herk's stock-block was superior to A. J.'s own killer Watson Offy 220. This led to tension and more amazing races. Especially the one in summer of 1961, when Herkie first ran away from Parnelli, and next forced A. J. to fight so hard that Foyt ultimately demolished his Offy. That fluorescent orange V-8 of Herk's just bombed on and on and none of Herk's other five-in-a-row Terre Haute scores was so epic.

At Ascot Park's annual fall USAC sprint match of 1962, I watched Herk win while flying blind through fog that surely was just as thick as the dust of Minot. And then suddenly descending through the swirling mist came, of all things, a helicopter. Herk, you see, was only getting warmed up: he couldn't even visit the Dorrick to go celebrate because he wasn't done racing.

The whirlybird was his chartered lift to the Salton Sea where he had a pressing engagement at a crackerbox speedboat marathon in the morning. I suppose the real surprise was that he wasn't doing the flying himself,

A. J. Foyt and Parnelli Jones. Parnelli went on record describing A. J. as the best of them all. *Bob Tronolone*

because he had his own war surplus seaplane. It was an old crumbling rattletrap—so shaky that not even Herk's German shepherd liked to go up in it. One time Parnelli did, though, and he later reported how Herk landed on a lake, where a man came running up, yelling, "Fools! Fools! This lake is filled with stumps!" And with a flash of the Hurtubise orbs, and the trademark laugh, Herk retorted, "Screw you, mister. I land here all the time!"

"Was there ever *anybody* like Herk?" Don Shepherd once asked, inadvertently forgetting Wally Campbell. Devouring-eyed and crazy-with-racing Jim Hurtubise was so unique, in fact, that all along he may have been racing with the wrong tribe. Instead of fighting it out on the often grim dirt track highway, might he have made a better fit down in the Deep South with the merry Flock brothers, Tim and Fronty, who used to race taxicabs wearing Bermuda shorts and with a live Rhesus monkey in the car? Or with bellylaughing Little Joe Weatherly and Pops Turner and their preppy saddle shoes, aloha shirts, and doll babies? Or with all the rest of that talented, rollicking, fruitcake army who invented stock car racing?

• • •

Parnelli raced hard and his driving style looked it; Herkie made dirt racing look like it was dangerous fun; A. J. Foyt's style said, forget everyone else, this is the way a dirt track driver is supposed to look. Those were

Foyt became 1951–1971's irreplaceable name by going fast in anything and winning everywhere. He just didn't feel as if he was living up to his talents unless he was winning on the bricks of Indy one Sunday and, say, the hummocks of Langhorne the next. And then strapping himself to a midget at Terre Haute. And then dizzily climbing up the slants of Salem in a sprinter. And then attacking at hurtling speed through the Pacific Coast fog at Ascot. Still the great one wasn't done. As the most exalted shoe going, occasionally A. J. had to go race in the taxicab Deep South. When the occasion demanded, he'd even go and win some international sports car match. *Bob Tronolone*

some wonderful race drivers we had in 1951–1971, and those of us lucky enough to see them dug them all, but, as Parnelli himself once said, the greatest was A. J.

Yet in one sense Foyt was negative. In his prime—and with the notable exception of Rodger Ward—he seemed to have others so buffaloed just going in that even those who liked to consider themselves Foyt's most fanatical adversaries—Bobby Marshman, say—frequently looked like they were paralyzed from intimidation. For example, at the 1964 Springfield where Foyt was leading, I watched Marshman in second place in a superior car have A. J. dead to rights with 10 miles' worth of opportunities on a perfect track for passing. Yet no pass occurred, and it wasn't strictly because of A. J.'s driving.

Foyt grew up believing in the power of Tony Bettenhausen, and like Tony began his rite of passage in midgets, first in A. J.'s native Texas, later throughout

the Southwest, and then the Midwest. By 1956—two years before Herk got there, three years before Parnelli—A. J. was racing sprints with the IMCA. Two experiences there hardened him. At the Minnesota State Fair, he had to go to fist city with Jack Jordon, a superstitious giant out of L.A.; and out on the Kansas plains, on the sixth lap of a heat race, A. J. got up close and personal with the marble orchard for the first and only time during a violent altercation between himself and Don Hutchinson, which Hutchinson, previously a spectacular flat-track biker, didn't survive.

In May of 1957, A. J. won his first USAC midget feature at Olympic Stadium in Kansas City—Jud Larson's old track. Not long afterwards, Wally Meskowski gave him his first ride on a sprinter slant track. A. J. had his next encounter with well-seasoned Rodger Ward. It was an encounter with consequences on both their careers and dirt racing.

One of L.A.'s original midget Offy troopers, Rodger was in the process of finding himself again after acquiring the dubious nickname of "Rodger the Dodger" for dodging death despite his involvement in the same wrecks that did in Clay Smith and Billy Vukovich. A terrific dirt tracker, Rodger was also a slick sandbagger and not above screwing up the heads of opponents by getting inside their brains. Young A. J. well knew all this, yet still went to Rodger asking which of two vehicles open to him he should race in 1957's Springfield 100, A. J.'s dirt champ car debut. Probably for the first and only time, Rodger gave A. J. the information straight. So A. J., naturally not wishing to have Rodger think he'd just fallen off a hay truck, rejected Rodger's choice and chose the other sled, the elderly *Hoover Motor Express*.

Time trials commenced. Qualifying fourth fastest, Ward sat on the outside hole of Springfield's second row. Moments before the start, A. J. accosted him.

"Guess I showed you," said A. J.

"What do you mean?" asked Rodger.

Helpful Tony Bettenhausen just couldn't stay out of a buddy's ailing car. *Bob Tronolone*

Upside-Down Rounds earned his nickname perhaps a dozen times. At last, fed up at having little to show for his work but bruises and bumps, he gave dirt racing a final shot in the summer of 1961 by towing a brand-new Hank Henry sprinter from L.A. back to the Terre Haute Action Track. Determined to avoid trouble this time, Upside-Down deliberately ran dead-last until he could see the waving checkered flag. Certain that no harm could possibly befall him now, Upside-Down almost reluctantly uncoiled his throttle foot and drew slowly abreast of the car ahead as if it were his mortal enemy. The box arbitrarily changed directions and Upside-Down unavoidably clipped its rear wheel and launched himself again; characteristically, he took his last checkered tumbling end-over-end. Later he took up skydiving with a vengeance. *Bob Tronolone*

Johnny Rutherford in 1962, his first campaign on USAC's champ car and sprinter dirt highway. *Bob Tronolone*

"I just bumped Pat O'Connor in the car you told me to drive, and I was in the car you told me not to."

"Listen, sonny," replied Rodger, "if you'd have driven the one I told you to, you'd be starting up here instead of the last row."

"Says you."

"That piece of junk you're in won't last long enough for me to lap you."

"Let's bet. How much?"

And A. J.'s was indeed one of the first cars Ward doubled while winning the 100 in record time. But he purposely delayed lapping the *Hoover* until everybody was coming down the main straight. Consequently, the grandstands observed A. J. receiving Rodger's digital "salute"—a gesture that A. J. never forgave or forgot. For the rest of both men's careers, A. J. raced against Rodger as if he were on some special mission to beat him, to really stick it to him. In turn, Rodger, whenever he could, responded by making A. J. work the hardest for what he got. He was even tougher on A. J. than Parnelli and Herk.

In 1958–1959, continuing his climb, A. J. got the chair in the *Dean Van Lines Special*, Jimmy Bryan's old ride, and, along with it, Bryan's savvy chief mechanic Clint Brawner. Clint saw to it that A. J. made the show at the 1958 Indy—the dirt highway had worked again—and he helped orchestrate Foyt's next big moment, this one at Langhorne, where on the last lap A. J. overwhelmed Jud Larson and took him for second place.

George Bignotti must have noticed the pass, too, plus other things, because in 1960 he took Foyt away from Dean and Brawner for himself. For the following four campaigns—except those times when George and A. J. were feuding—the Bignotti-Foyt juggernaut at Bowes Seal-Fast and later Sheraton-Thompson subsequently took full command of champ car dirt racing and racing generally. A. J. won the USAC seasonal titles of 1960 and 1961—1961 also being the season of Foyt's iconical midget ride at Terre Haute—and even when A. J.'s old friend Ward wrestled the national crown away in 1962, all it did was put A. J. in a mood to make Rodger pay for it. In 1963, winner of five of a dozen races and champion again, A. J. clobbered Ward by better than 700 points. Still inspired and angry in 1964, A. J. unleashed perhaps the most amazing season anyone has ever had, winning all five dirt 100s and five of the eight paved meets plus his second Indy 500.

Incredibly, he might have additionally become USAC champion of sprints and midgets—he led their

point standings at times, too—if only there'd been enough open weekends. Now I kick myself for not paying more attention to A. J. throughout 1964. The opportunity of getting to see the very best when he *is* the very best is rare; and to me A. J. was never the same A. J. after a ruinously serious wreck in January of 1965. His Banjo Mathews doorslammer lost its brakes at a NASCAR road meet in California and went tumbling to the bottom of Riverside Raceway's turn nine canyon, leaving A. J. in mean pain with a smashed back.

Bobby, Johnny, and Mario

So the 1950s ended and the 1960s kicked in. But in the matter of reaching the Brickyard via the dirt track highway vs. visiting the marble orchard, it was almost a stalemate. Or maybe the marble orchard was even in the lead.

The body count was impossible. You could start with some of the big ones taken out *after* they'd successfully hit the 500 and become winners, pole position-sitters, rookies of the year: Jimmy Bryan, Johnny Thomson, Bill Schindler, Jack McGrath, Walt Faulkner, Jerry Hoyt, Crash Crockett . . .

Drop your guard for a fraction of a second, yonder the marble orchard! Jack McGrath, despite being employed by an Indy car owner who was a rich oilie with one of the biggest pokes in racing—he'd have bought Jack anything he wanted—decided to be stingy with his racing budget and not buy a new axle for his Kurtis-Kraft; the defective old axle snapped and set Jack headlong down the back-straight at Phoenix. Mike Nazaruk, the battling leatherneck and Langhorne luminary, was paying more attention to settling accounts with Charlie Musselman than to racing, so Langhorne

Mario Andretti took a long route to the top: from a displaced persons camp in Italy, to a racing program sponsored by that country; to an uncle's house in Nazareth, Pennsylvania, and the grandstand at Langhorne. From there, he got himself into a driver's seat, put his foot down, and never let up.
Dan Mahony

Don Branson learned his trade in the iron 1950s, then spent the early and middle 1960s passionately standing up to the onslaughts of advancing age and the new kids: Johnny, Mario, and Bobby Unser. Often faster than they were, he missed their stamina. When 1966 arrived, five USAC men at arms got the chop in five months, including Don. That was the end of the dirt track highway. Nobody in their right mind wanted to get on it anymore, and Johnny, Mario, Bobby, and others all reluctantly abandoned USAC sprints. *Bob Tronolone*

rose up and bit him. Shorty Templeman, at the end of his tether after losing his Indy car ride, went to a penny-ante midget show on a horrible track and blitzed himself and another driver. Art Bisch touched the wall at Atlanta and damaged his car, continued racing anyway, then paid with "all of it" the next lap when the car fell apart. Jim Packard, who wouldn't take "no" for an answer and maybe was braver than his talents, finally had his overachieving backfire when his midget turned five cartwheels. Joie James had made himself king of the slant tracks, had young Mari Hulman for a girlfriend, and nothing ahead of him but blue skies and more checkereds. That is, until an especially idiotic wreck during a yellow-flag condition in blinding sunshine ended it all.

Ignoring your own premonitions appeared to be another ticket to the marble orchard. Van Johnson, a pallbearer at the funeral of a racing bud, told his car owner Ed Lowther that one day Lowther would be putting him, Van, in such a box, too; it happened barely two months later. Jimmy Reece, who saw his friends disappear and got on everyone's nerves telling them they were going to be next, instead got it himself. Jack Jordon, who had slugged it out with A. J. Foyt at the Minnesota State Fair, tried setting a track record in a midget, crashed and failed, yet achieved his superstitious wish of getting planted in the city where he expired: Phoenix.

Maybe the unluckiest dirt track highway victims were those who didn't go cleanly. Bobby Ball banged his head in a midget and lay unconscious for 14 months before succumbing. Lee Wallard, just days after winning the 1951 Indy, felt his sprint car spraying him with fuel from a jammed carburetor float, chose to take a chance and not stop, then never could race again after the car lit up with himself trapped and burning inside. Asbestos Andy Linden, who'd survived the heat at Indy and getting run over on the track at Syracuse, had the ragged carpet of a midget track put him on his nob, and ended up getting spinal taps and living in a wheelchair—being a hard-on hadn't been a guarantee from the ravages of the marble garden after all. (Years later, ever true to character, slugging Andy was said to have raised a big paw from his wheelchair to cold-cock the racing promoter who'd built the offending track surface.)

Yet the marble orchard could be capricious. It didn't, for instance, take so obvious a candidate as Upside-Down Rounds, whose whole career was spent overturning and clobbering trackscape from Imperial to

Reading. But Upside-Down was unimpressed with his good fortune and upon finally retiring from the dirt highway took up skydiving with a vengeance; he survived that as well.

Unfortunately, anyone imagining that conditions on the dirt highway were going to be tamer and safer in the 1960s was in for a disappointment, because the marble orchard remained voracious. May of 1961 at Indy saw "Panzerman" Tony Bettenhausen turn himself into a test-driver guinea pig and never return from his test. June saw Wayne Weiler get too close to Herk Hurtubise at Terre Haute, flip many times, and absorb career-concluding injuries. October saw Al Keller end his days at Phoenix.

None of this gore and mayhem deterred fresh enlistees on the dirt track highway who knew they were immune from its ravages. The 1950s had been Parnelli's, Herk's, and A. J.'s deal, as well as, mainly, an L.A. deal. But now it was the 1960s and Indy aspirants like Bobby Unser, Johnny Rutherford, and Mario Andretti from other geographical regions expected their shots.

In the case of Bobby Unser—as well as most of the other superstimulated members of the Unser clan of Albuquerque, New Mexico—it was more like an ongoing shot. Mere mention of the Unsers seems to make the marble orchard rev up with interest. Two of Bobby's dirt track highway forebears—an uncle way back in the 1920s, and an older brother who ate it during the 1959 Indy practice—were already there.

Bobby's early life was blissfully spent on the ragged edge. He had inherited the family heavy foot: as a teenager he was in the center of fierce disputes at city hardtop shows. Adventures he experienced in the old Mexican Road Race were of the life-and-death variety, and along with the family heavy foot he'd inherited the Unser passion for the hill climb up the sheer wall of 3-mile-high Pikes Peak, where one slip sent you tumbling into the wide blue void.

You can make a reputation taking risks, so early on Bobby seemed to be on a trajectory to the Brickyard over the dirt track highway. Thanks to the networking of John Laux, the mayor of the White Front saloon, Bobby at the end of the 1950s had midget, sprint, and dirt champ car rides lined up if only he could safely make it out of Albuquerque to the Midwest. He failed. Stopping in Tulsa to visit the John Zink racing team, he noticed some of Jack Zink's friends playing with a hot go-kart and the race driver couldn't resist showing the civilians how to ride the thing. With a split-second to

Mario on his early midget and sprint car dirt tracking: "A beginning driver is bound to be coarse as hell because he hasn't learned any other way to race yet. And not knowing how to race the proper way, he may automatically do it the wrong way . . . It's what's called 'Making your bones.'" *Bob Tronolone*

Mario and the old Eddie Sachs *Dean Van Lines* Kuzma slowly cook the right rear—all to no avail. A. J. Foyt came on to win this 1968 Sacramento 100, his fifth career 100 on the California mile. *Bob Tronolone*

sort things out after the throttle stuck, Bobby didn't do a good job and KO'd himself sledgehammering a brick building. Baby brother Al had to come out to drive him home, and when they got back to Albuquerque, brain fluid was leaking out of Bobby's ears.

Catching mono during his recuperation turned him into a medical basket case, but only briefly, and soon Bobby was back on the job popping stay-awake pills while campaigning midgets and sprinters all over New Mexico, Arizona, and California. Given anything with a rumbling big engine and halfway decent tread on its shoes, he was unbeatable; even when jockeying a shitbox he continued racing as if the dirt driver with the biggest foot made all the rules. Car owners loved him, but kamikaze strategy also had real marble orchard

potential, and so, for an insurance policy, Bobby brought in Tilt Millican. Before allowing Bobby to strap into his latest deathmobile, Tilt gave it the Albuquerque double-howdy, which meant watchdogging so that at least all four wheels were on tight.

By 1963, Bobby was back on trajectory to Indy, qualifying for his first 500 in, almost appropriately, one of the hexed and monster V-8 Bull Novis. And all its supercharged rolling thunder and hell-fire yodeling didn't deter him from drilling the wall inside of two laps. Didn't take him long at all.

•   •   •

In that same 500 as Bobby, making his own arrival courtesy of the dirt track highway, was Johnny Rutherford.

Born in Kansas, raised in Texas, he saw his first midget race at 10, became a hot rod club member in his teens, and way before he could vote was part of the Dallas blue-collar mob who kicked the windows out of their Ford flatheads and manhandled them as econoclass bolides at Devil's Bowl.

Johnny's education on the dirt thoroughfare commenced on the battlefields of the IMCA cornstalk tour. It was his destiny to be linked with interesting cars, including one of Diz Wilson's 14-year-old beauties, which happened to be all that was left of the original Pat Clancy six-wheeler. Then later on in 1962, Johnny was aboard a bulbous and high-sided yellow rig complete with killer motor that wallowed through everything and raised enough dirt to knock paint off cars it passed. Don Shepherd, its mechanic, had it well tuned to eat up fairgrounds races and seldom had to lift the hood except to clean the radiator or dump in 20 percent nitro, glug-glug.

Driver and mechanic looked like the hot ticket to win IMCA's seasonal title until Johnny and Shep got crossways with each other about whether Johnny should interrupt their operations to make his bow as a USAC gladiator at the Hoosier Hundred. Breaking up acrimoniously when Johnny decided to, Shep acquired a demon sprint car—formerly Elmer George's—to resume being an outlaw, and Johnny headed to the Indiana State Fair. Ironically, his Hoosier ride was the same *Bell Lines Trucking* that Shep's sibling A. J. had used the year before to try to knock down all the barns of the fairgrounds. Johnny successfully qualified—he was uncompetitive in the Hoosier Hundred itself—but for him the beauty was that the seat in Bell's Watson roadster for the 1963 Indy went with the deal.

Then Smokey Yunick, the wizard of taxicab NASCAR, unexpectedly telephoned. Another planet

A. J. works the dirt. Mile-track grooves constantly changed in the course of 100 miles. Finding the fast line took wisdom. To win his aforementioned fifth Sacramento 100, A. J. started out on top (top left), then manipulated the middle (top right), and at last came down to the inside pole (above). *Bob Tronolone*

heard from. Needing to glom on to somebody hot and fresh to gas his backdoor factory porcupine Chevrolet in Daytona Beach's February 500, Smokey—himself wise to the potency of the dirt track highway—wondered if Johnny harbored prejudices against doorslammers.

Johnny did not—even though the open-cockpit midget, sprint, and dirt car varsity classified stock car racing as something you did when you retired from real racing. He went to Daytona, climbed up on big D's high bankings to qualify at 165.181 miles per hour, won a preliminary 100-miler, and was smack in the middle of the fight in the stocker 500 until he had to spin himself out of a tank-slapper and lost two laps in the pits having Smokey cut off a splattered right-rear quarter panel.

May's Indy 500 was a comedown in speed of almost 20 miles per hour, yet still INN-DEE-AN-APP-POH-LUS! Reaching the end of the dirt track highway and snagging a starting hole in the Big One amounted to Johnny's mega-moment, even though he was back on the ninth row and had to go through two tired roadsters to get there. With 157 laps still to come, he was already done with a ruptured tranny.

Then he spent the rest of 1963 taking bold if inconclusive drives out on the mile tracks of the championship trail in still another most interesting chariot, the *J. H. Rose Chevy*. A "gasket car" amidst all the Offenhausers—and one with a generous cubic-inch advantage—the big-but-fragile *Rose* had a horrendous appetite for rocker arms: it ate one at Springfield after Johnny had time-trialed on the front row. And on the green flag of the Hoosier Hundred, Johnny and the *Rose* were out-gambited by ever-cunning old Rodger Ward and the *Leader Card*. Backing off for turn one just when Johnny did, Rodger unexpectedly jumped back on the throttle again. Courtesy of a big slide act that made the *Leader Card* brush the fence, Rodger then went to full warp and led all 100 miles.

The same Ward stratagems didn't work out at Sacramento—this time Johnny totally blew off the *Leader Card* getting into one—but later the *Rose* caught the outside fence just where a bolt was sticking out and it took out the steering.

Over the winter, Don Shepherd ended his outlaw poaching of other sprinter regions and Johnny returned to Shep's life as driver of Shep's Elmer car.

In Ohio the following spring, on the Eldora Speedway dirt hills, the team won its first USAC main event.

Above and right: Johnny Rutherford and Bobby Unser, two matriculates of the Don Shepherd sprint car school, learned their lessons well, going on to grab half a dozen Indy 500 wins between them. *Bob Tronolone*

But just when Johnny and Shep were looking like a team to watch, Johnny, at the 1964 Indy, got caught up in the seven-driver catastrophe and fire on the second lap that carried off two more drivers to the marble orchard, one of them Eddie Sachs.

One of the other drivers besides Johnny who was involved in the disaster was Bobby Unser, whose rolling thunder Novi had blasted through the smoke and flame—Bobby's neck got roasted—only to put itself on the fritz ramming Johnny's *Bardahl* roadster. Cooked neck notwithstanding, Bobby wanted back into the 500 in the worst way, so he solved the neck problem by cracking open a can of 50 weight with a church key to slap lubricant on the wounds. But he couldn't solve the problem of getting back into the race because of his failure to coerce car owners to fire their existing drivers in favor of himself.

The 1964 summer passed and it was one of the worst, what with Johnny White's getting lamed at Terre Haute and the could-have-been-fatal methanol burning of Herk on the Milwaukee pavement. And, as they invariably did, teams were falling apart. The Johnny-Shep sprint car tandem, for one, came hard aground, leaving Johnny a pedestrian and Shep in the market for a shoe. All the other USAC teams were ripe for the taking, Shep was certain, if only he could find the right one.

Bobby was under consideration, but the Shep-Bobby mating dance was to be protracted. At first he thought Bobby might have something he could use, but after keeping a mental dossier of all the mistakes he thought he saw Bobby committing in sprint cars, Shep was thinking, "Forget that."

Conversely, if there was one owner of a sprint car Bobby was avoiding, it was Shep. He knew he ran a moving and hard-tackling team, but he also knew all about Shep's hiring only drivers with flame in their tummies. He'd heard all the horror stories of Shep getting crabby and firing drivers during hot laps—before the real racing even started—because in Shep's estimation they weren't pushing the button diligently enough. Shep's drivers sometimes got waved into the pits and told they were canned while a race was still going on! And yet because no driver had ever been seriously busted up in a Shep car, and because Shep was a secret sentimentalist who didn't want something like that on his conscience, there was a catch-22 paradox. Shep routinely fired drivers for racing like zombies, yet he also fired them if they scared him by overextending themselves.

Johnny Rutherford and the sportin' life of the IMCA! At the 1961 Minnesota State Fair, Hershell Wagner lunched a mill and set off a major traffic jam by slowing abruptly. Straight into the parking lot hauled JR, who had no opportunity to miss hitting Russ Long and subsequently had to airmail his *Diz Wilson Special*, the former *Pat Clancy* six-wheeler. *Al Herman, Johnny Rutherford collection*

Finally, Shep and Bobby did get together, at New Bremen, an Ohio half-mile that was a long haul from Albuquerque. The only way Bobby could get back there was by air, and the old banger he was flying in those years was about as sanitary as the infamous Hurtubise seaplane. Bobby being Bobby, most of his piloting adventures were legend: once, after they somehow managed to land Bobby's banger right-side-up, Bobby's passenger, Roger McCluskey, bailed out to kiss the ground in gratitude.

Anyway, Bobby flew back to New Bremen, and there was no Shep. Everybody had been racing over east the night before and Shep's Elmer car had been in a crash and never made it back. So Bobby landed a substitute ride with the *Steve Stapp Special*.

Suddenly, the Shep outfit belatedly came rolling in, the Elmer car a mass of bent iron including twisted radius rods, exhaust headers stoved in, and messed-up front axle.

Up ran Shep, a bad look on his face. "Bobby, I hear you got Stapp's car to run!"

"No, I told Stapp that if you showed, I'd run you."

"Mine's still beat up. Might not handle."

"Well, you want to run it?"

"Well, you want to drive it?"

"Can you have it ready for second warm-up sessions?"

"Yup."

"Get that sumbitch ready."

Fifty-three spoken words, and they led to a bonding. To make the Elmer car perform, Bobby had to jujitsu it, but only Don Branson could beat him. Afterward, asking Shep how he'd done, Shep said, "Not too bad"—a giant compliment, coming from Shep. And when Bobby confessed that he wasn't sure he could ever keep up with Branson again, Shep's reply was sharp: "I certainly hope you can. We've got to race him again next week."

They shouldn't have gotten along at all. Bobby was Hurtubise-like in preferring to engineer his own sleds, but Shep, who ran the tightest ship in racing, wouldn't tolerate that. And although Shep never praised Bobby for doing an exceptional job, he'd regularly go into bitter detail about all his mistakes, plus deliver smiling and deadly analyses of Bobby's other shortcomings. Even so, Bobby warmed to Shep in an extraordinary way.

Normally one of the most penny-pinching of all drivers, Bobby instructed Shep not to pay him the customary 50 percent of the purse whenever they won, but

4

7

5

8

6

9

RUTHERFORD
CEDAR RAPIDS
1972-?

JR wins again. Left to right, Johnny, Frank Winkley of the IMCA, and the great Shep. *Les Burianek, Jake Bozony collection*

instead to plow the bonus 10 percent into upkeep. The reason? Hard as Bobby raced, Shep himself seemed to work far harder making miracles from the pits. Shep absolutely refused to quit. If, say, Bobby dropped a cylinder, he was under orders never to shut down but to keep standing on it regardless, even if the whole block got honeycombed. Never quit! Maybe something would happen and they'd still win. Bobby related well to such a philosophy.

• • •

Shep could not believe his eyes. It was late 1964, and he and Bobby were in the south of Indiana for the 100-lapper at paved Salem Speedway. Bobby, who'd earlier run out of brakes, was having a long, difficult day on the tall walls; Shep, watching, was figuratively riding along with his boy and sharing every swerve and dart. But then a blue *Gapco Special*, leading the race and lapping the field, caught Bobby straddling the fast groove. It rended him into the fence, then proceeded on about its business!

The *Gapco* ended up in the winners circle. So did Shep. Not one to take the wrecking of the Elmer car or the roughing up of Bobby lightly, Shep weighed in with an ass-chewing of the Gapco's little driver—who immediately interrupted Shep by snapping back that Marquess of Queensbury niceties didn't apply and that Shep should either put better brakes on the Elmer car or else tell Bobby to keep out of the bleeping way of faster drivers.

Tough monkey. It was Mario Gabriel Andretti.

Here's a five-ingredient recipe for anybody grooming himself to be Race Driver of the Century: 1) be born during wartime on a forlorn chunk of real estate that Yugoslavia, Austria, and Italy have been squabbling over for eons; 2) grow up in abject poverty in a displaced persons camp in Italy after the forlorn chuck of real estate gets ceded to Yugoslavia and a commie regime at the end of World War II; 3) participate strictly on the quiet with your younger (by six hours) twin brother in a race driver-training program subsidized by the Italian government; 4) get uprooted all over again when your mother's uncle in Nazareth, Pennsylvania, in the blue-collar steel belt, sponsors you to America as immigrants; and 5) witness your very first U.S. race at Langhorne—enough to blow anybody's mind—which inspires both you and your twin, Aldo, to jump on the dirt track highway.

Aldo fell by the wayside, but Mario clawed his way up through modified stocks, indoor buzzbomb TQ minimidgets, and at last the full-size midgets of the ARDC. Hungry to make ink, on the Labor Day weekend of 1963 Mario sped across P-A and Jersey to win three midget main events on two different tracks in one day, something only Shorty Templeman had ever done before, and the exploit had almost broken the dwarf Shorty. Accomplishing it, Mario afterward felt like he was "made."

He wasn't; he was only getting started on the dirt highway. A wild rookie USAC sprint car gun in 1964, he was nerve-racking to be around. Down in the first corner at New Bremen, when someone ahead did something that Mario wasn't expecting, Mario delivered a torpedoing, causing two cars behind him to wreck and subject their respective drivers to a braining and an arm amputation. With 20 laps to go at Allentown, Mario, in 11th place, set out to catch A. J. Foyt the leader, accomplishing it in 14 laps. But A. J. knew how to get rid of him. Putting up with Mario for only four laps, A. J. rode him in deep, made him spin out, and innocent bystander Don Branson cracked up missing him.

Now at Salem, Mario had acquainted himself with Bobby and Shep. And throughout 1965 the two friends—incredible as it sounds, Mario and Bobby became friends,

"Everybody who races a sprint car has to get nicked, to fall by the wayside," said Bobby Unser. Well, he knew. *Bob Tronolone*

though Mario and Shep never quite did—kept smacking
themselves around in everything from Indy Funny Cars at
Trenton to sprinters at Ascot. It wasn't deliberate; they just
couldn't stay out of one another's way. But it was epic
sprint car racing anyway. Don Branson, winner of the
1964 championship despite injuries, was beside himself
keeping up with all the fast young cats coming off the dirt
highway: not just Mario but Greg Weld, Red Reigel,
Scratch Daniels, Arnie Knepper, and Mickey Rupp. Roger
McCluskey was back in form with his old *Konstant Hot
Special* after his miracle year in 1963; and Jud Larson was
also on full-comeback mode.

But what turned out to be the 1965 campaign's
crucial moment occurred not on dirt but as an aftermath to a mid-season eruption on the paving at Indianapolis Raceway Park. A. J. Foyt was there to make a

celebrity sprinter appearance in Wally Meskowski's *No. 9*,
an unusual bent-springer crafted by Eddie Kuzma.
Despite being old colleagues, A. J. and Wally managed to
embroil themselves in a huge disagreement about how
No. 9 was or wasn't performing.

Although not as big as A. J., Wally could have
just as angry a voice when pushed. Additionally,
Wally was Shep-like in knowing he was never wrong,
and just like any other sprint car builder-owner-
mechanic it often seemed to Wally that his whole life
was a big running battle with race drivers, including
cleaning up their messes. Wally believed the saying,
"A race driver's brain is in his foot" was a positive
instead of a negative adage because it suggested that a
race driver actually had a brain. This was something
doubted by other owner/mechanics, particularly Jud

Phillips, employer of Don Branson, who once famously said, "Race drivers are like leaves on trees—they're everywhere."

All this notwithstanding, Wally, Shep, and Jud continued on as passionate racers anyway, and their ogre philosophies and dictatorial methods really worked and were responsible for schooling all 1951–1971 Indy 500 winners.

Yet Wally—even more than Shep or Jud—was on record as declaring that if any so-and-so race driver

ever tried getting tough with him, he'd give him his toughness right back. So, right at the peak of the Foyt/Wally disagreement, Wally, wearing a borrowed helmet, was first observed furiously strapping himself into *No. 9*, and next observed attempting to coerce a pick-up truck into pushing him out onto IRP to demonstrate to A. J. and the world that *nothing* was the matter with *No. 9*. Wally, with no previous race driver experience, was guaranteeing he could lap within a second of A. J.'s time.

Dick Atkins with the *Agajanian* Kuzma takes on leader Mario Andretti in the *Dean Van Lines* Kuzma at 1966's Sacramento 100. The two were also teammates on the Wally Meskowski sprint car squad. This time Mario popped and Dick—with less than a month to live—won. *Bob Tronolone*

Shep was one of those watching the incident who was disappointed Wally wasn't allowed to go through with it, because he thought Wally might have succeeded. Where was it written that a sprint car owner couldn't race just as fast as his moron race driver? Watching for a different reason was Johnny Rutherford, whose career, compared to those of Bobby's and Mario's, was in something of a stall. During IRP hotlaps he'd piled up his latest ride, Steve Stapp's car, and Stapp had sacked him. Helmet in hand, Johnny now went to Wally about taking over his vacant *No. 9* and Wally growled OK.

Their first race together was a week or so later on a wet surface at Eldora, where *No. 9* was really hooked up on the bottom and Johnny cut the nighttime competition to pieces. Bobby and Shep then proceeded to win three straight. Greg Weld also went on a tear. But Johnny and Wally went back to winning. Out at Ascot in the season finale, A. J. Foyt and Bobby knocked each other out in a tangle, and Johnny and Wally—despite *No. 9* throwing two different wheels in the same awkward race— were knighted national sprint car champions.

The 1966 tourney was bound to be yet another ripper.

• • •

Wally Meskowski realized how lucky he was. It was 3 A.M. on an October Sunday on highway 101, the big artery from L.A. to Frisco, and Wally, towing his *No. 9* to the afternoon show at Altamont Speedway, had been stopped twice for speeding by the same California Highway Patrol cruiser. The first time Wally had gotten off with a warning; the second time the chippie had let him off too. For Wally this was an amazing break in a season that hadn't caught many—including the hell of Ascot just a few hours earlier.

The year that was destined to see the marble orchard take out five drivers in only eight months, including two of dirt's living legends, had kicked off at Reading amidst the greatest anticipation yet. But outsiders must have wondered what was going on. Why were the likes of Johnny, Bobby, Mario, Roger McCluskey, and Don Branson still riding the dirt highway in sprinters? Having all become regular starters and even near-winners of the Indy 500, they had long since accomplished their goals on dirt. And it wasn't as if sprint car racing paid a lot of prize money; it didn't. All of them could have done better being P.R. shills for some corporation. For that matter, what was a successful Indy 500 wrench like Jud Phillips, chief mechanic for Branson, still doing campaigning a sprint? Jud had done the

Mario explores the rim. *Bob Tronolone*

arithmetic and computed that even if his team won the sprinter championship, the best he, Branson, and their assistant, Little Red Herman, could do was break even.

But the insiders knew. It wasn't about money. With a cast like John, Bobby, Mario, Roger, and Don, dirt track sprinters had turned into the hottest circuit going—and if you were a real racer, it had become the place to be. Even Mario, by now an international celebrity, had flown all night from the Sebring just to be at Reading for the 1966 opener.

Established as the squad to chase, Wally Meskowski's two-car team instead floundered at Reading. The new *No. 1* Wally had built for Johnny wasn't right and Mario in Johnny's old *No. 9* lost to Jud Larson.

Come the next gray Sunday at Eldora, Johnny was again struggling; speeding past the pits he sought tutelage, and Wally responded with the "move higher" sign.

Johnny moved. To his annoyance, all he discovered were broken ruts; meantime additional drivers shot past on the inside.

Now steering with one hand, he vigorously waved the middle finger of the other at Wally, after which he raised his face shield—perhaps in a vain attempt for better insight. What he got instead was a rock the size of a baseball thrown up by Mario's tire, which caught Johnny full on the kisser. Upon awakening some time afterward, Johnny found himself outside Eldora in a shallow creek bed with *No. 1* on top of him. Both his arms were pulverized from the effects of three wailing end-over-ends and Johnny was out for the season.

Racing went on; so did its costs. Back at Reading in June, Jud Larson, well past his prime, was pressing. Flat busted again, it was time to start making some loot. Jud put his *Dunseth Special* on the front row and when his mechanic, Paul Leffler, asked how he was going to keep it there in the race, Jud offered his standard, "Turn it backwards in the first corner and be gone." This was the night Jud threw his last broadside. His Dunseth got hung up in the cushion just as Red Riegel came roaring in all committed. Their tangled-up cars rolled off the track, came back on, stopped upside down, and both of them were gone.

Racing still went on. The tournament carried everyone from Indiana and Pennsylvania and back

Mile-track 100s were fiendishly difficult competitions to win. Bobby Unser won practically everywhere else, yet never in a champ car on a dirt mile.
Bob Tronolone

again, and some of the winners were Bobby and Mario and occasionally Branson, Larry Dickson, and Arnie Knepper. But Roger McCluskey was beginning to have a dominating year like that of 1963.

The marble orchard struck again in Kansas City. Working the guardrail of Olympic Stadium and coming on an outside flier from 11th to 4th, Ron Lux got in the way of himself and tried something that didn't work on Arnie Knepper. Arnie escaped, but Ron took a fatal flip.

Everybody tried to forget it as best they could at Tulsa, Oklahoma, and then the next race in Merle Haggard country at Muskogee's Thunderbird Speedway gave drivers a slimy, wet battleground of red clay so

slick that even the wheel-packing rigs were smacking into each other.

Everybody was guessing about tires—diamond treads vs. Lightning Drags—but the meet was to be marked by what seemed to be an epic Shep/Bobby meltdown. So far they'd had a good swing. Bobby had set a new track record qualifying at K.C. and had been second in the feature, then set another fast time at Tulsa and had taken fifth. But now something happened between Bobby and Mario. Shep had Bobby practicing on Lightning Drags, and they seemed to be the hot tip. But when Mario stopped by to ask how they were working—exchanging rubber info was routine—Bobby replied, "Aw, Mario, not worth a damn."

Jud Larson holding things straight instead of sideways for a change. Judging from the expression on the Larson mug, he's not enjoying it.
Bob Tronolone

Mario left and Shep asked Bobby, "What'd you lie to him for?" Bobby shrugged and answered "Aw, Shep, it'll be OK."

"It's going to be a long night," Shep retorted.

Never fond of Mario after the early set-to at Salem, Shep still objected to Bobby's giving him bad information. Shep's soft conscience always made him afraid of someone getting hurt. What if Mario listened to Bobby and put on the wrong tires and busted his butt? How would they feel?

Well, the whole thing backfired anyway. Lighting Drags turned out to be the wrong call—the impossible Muskogee surface at last came in perfect for diamonds. But for punishment, Shep deliberately made Bobby unsuccessfully continue running Lighting Drags through the first, second, and third qualifying heats. Finally they had hostile words about it, Shep told Bobby he was fired, then actually loaded the Elmer car onto its trailer. But Roger McCluskey worked the détente that reunited them. The dispute ended as quickly as it began. Shep hammered on some diamonds, jacked in some right rear weight, and Bobby won the final qualifying heat and then copped fourth in the feature.

There were more late-season stops at Reading, New Bremen, and Terre Haute. With Jud Larson gone, Branson at 46 was by far the old man of the field, but he took a midget to the Hut Hundred and won. And at

The cast of fabulous characters from page 48 mounted up for business.
Bob Tronolone

the Sacramento 100 he took a blazing trial lap but lost the 100 late to Dick Atkins.

In L.A. at Ascot's doubleheader, Roger McCluskey had already clinched the sprint title but won the first Saturday night anyway. Everybody else was just trying to get front ends to stick.

The second Saturday night was foggy and comprised a grab-bag field with one big surprise—A. J. Foyt in Lover Boy Hogle's old *Tamale Wagon* Offy.

Neck-and-neck battles raged all over Ascot, but never for first because Roger was long gone. Don Bran-

son was hunting down cars from the back. And for no discernible reason, Don rammed the first turn fence, sent planks flying, then landed upside-down on the track. Arriving at full screaming throttle with no place to go was Atkins in the Meskowski *No. 1* car, formerly raced by Johnny. There was a fiery pileup and Atkins and Don were both dead.

The race restarted after half an hour and Roger won again.

To this day, no one knows what made Branson break off from the main pack of cars and impact the wall.

Afterward there was no official inquiry, nobody asked many questions, and what callous SOBs all of us were.

No, that's not fair, and it's not even true. Mark it down more to 1951–1971's warlike traditions: when your buddy drops, you ask no questions, expect no mercy, and just carry on. If you were a dilettante who couldn't stomach the risks, go race or watch sporty cars.

The racing did go on. Wally Meskowski, for one, loaded up his remaining *No. 9*, then towed it all night to Altamont where A. J.—having reconciled with Wally after their old IRP clash—used it to win the main event.

And so 1966, the year that started so brightly, effectively ended the dirt track highway. No young drivers in their right minds would ever again aspire to become such vulnerable, doomed race drivers as the 1951–1971 lot. And Indianapolis no longer wanted dirt track– talent anyway. So, in the matter of the marble orchard vs. the Indy 500, the stone necropolis seemed to have won decisively. Only it hadn't really, because Parnelli, A. J., Bobby, Johnny, and Mario certainly had beaten it, the five of them ultimately becoming the champions of a dozen Indy 500s.

Über soldiers of the dirt track highway!

Meeting by chance at a 1982 dirt track race at Raceland Park in Denver, seasonal champion Roger McCluskey, Don Branson helpster Little Red Herman, and the author reflect back on wonderful, costly 1966. *Tom Davey, Scalzo collection*

Chapter 3

SLEDS, CHUGS, AND BOXES

One afternoon in 1990, speaking at his studio in Baltimore, Sal Scarpitta, an artist campaigning his own team of winged sprint cars on the outlaw dirt tracks of Maryland and Pennsylvania, talked about the wadding of one of his sprinters, and how so-called junk that is exterminated on a race track can be recycled into another existence. "The car crashed right where I was standing," Sal explained, "and I couldn't get my eyes off it. My sprint car! Smoking and steaming and fucked over good again. But the driver was unhurt. And there was something at least animated about an object, a race car, going through so much trauma to be part of the human existence—a machine that was raced, wrecked, and that somebody had walked away from unscathed. I really thought it was deserving of some dignity. So, one of the wings became part of a collection in Europe. It's crushed. It looks like a Mexican tamale. But on it is the name of Leo Castelli, my dealer—a name that belongs to the art world. And the wing exists with all the implications of today—not in a romantic way—because it's so rolled up."

Sal is a sculptor and painter, one of the world's most imaginative. Additionally, just like a good dirt track bad boy should, he'd had a lifetime of stirring up as much mischief and having as many adventures as anyone ever born. Unfortunately, his artist's approach wouldn't have worked so well in 1951–1971. What with there being so much action and so little money, the combination of operating a champ dirt, sprint, or midget team and turning a profit eluded almost everyone. Meaning that none of the era's noble sleds, chugs, or boxes were allowed to be throwaways, but had to continue racing on and on no matter what. Even after getting royally wrecked, as most did, their splintered bones couldn't be recycled into another existence and sent to the peace and quiet of some otherworldly museum.

If they were the real-deal goodies, any wounded bits of merchandise were picked over, magnafluxed, and put back to hard work. In 1955, for instance, after Jack McGrath's champ dirt car the *Hinkle Special* took all its endos at Phoenix, everybody mourned the Nitro Man for an appropriate time. But then, being practical and frugal, Jack's peers grew concerned about what was going to become of the *Hinkle's* choice Conze fittings, its Kuzma seat, and belly pans, etc.; fast-moving Clint Brawner of Dean Van Lines got to them first. And in 1956 at Salem Speedway, after Bob Sweikert flew out of control and crashed through the first corner's photographers' stand, everyone knew that Bob's crunched car, the Midwest's reigning champion, was tricked out to the max. The widow Sweikert was romantic, though, and, not wanting the remains cannibalized, ordered everything destroyed. Somehow the Halibrand rear end survived, plus a few other valuable bits; they subsequently

You could see anything and everything at Ascot Park in southern Los Angeles. For example, right in the middle of the Watts insurrection of 1965 you could be seated in the nighttime grandstands and watch Paul Jones—brother of Parnelli—flip his sprinter clear over the top of the Bite-Rite sign on the backstraight and at the same time behold the whole L.A. skyline in flames. Another highly memorable moment occurred in 1967 when A. J. Watson and A. J. Foyt dropped in with this screamer 32-valve Ford four-cam Watson. Winning the main event, Foyt serenaded the grandstands with shrieking high revs that split the L.A. night. *Dwight Vaccaro*

arching corners were propped up against tree-rimmed slopes. They were especially evil on equipment, far worse than dirt: getting a single corner wrong at a slant track was an experience often followed by a lethal swerve up the lip of the banking; a smash into, over, or through a flimsy crashwall; and an agonizing plunge of several stories to the ground. But, again, this was 1951–1971, where drivers got blitzed routinely; cars, as per the Sweikert, seldom.

Another vehicle in point was the *Agajanian 98 Jr.* A 1948 Kuzma, *98 Jr.*, courtesy of Troy Ruttman and Offy Einstein Clay Smith, pinned it on everyone coast to coast; it was the sprinter that did for Rutt what A. J. Watson's *Dart Kart* Offy 220 later did for A. J. Foyt. Then in 1951 *98 Jr.* took a classic slant track fall out of Winchester that should have done it to death the same way it did its substitute driver. It didn't, though, and *98 Jr.* was soon up and running again with boy genius Rutt back in its wheelhouse. But the steering must have been improperly repaired, because late in 1952 it fell apart at Cedar Rapids and *98 Jr.* took a long brutal ride that at last stopped with *98 Jr.* on top of Rutt. Rutt's career and private life crumbled afterward, and with its second heavy crash in a year, *98 Jr.* had now surely earned the privilege of being put to sleep.

Guess again. Foul memories and bad vibes notwithstanding, it still had its proud ancestry, especially over east where all the hay shakers of P-A remembered *98 Jr.* and Rutt as the mighty pair that on occasion had hung it on their man Tommy H. at Reading and Williams Grove. And however beaten up *98 Jr.* might be, still inside its screaming 220 were those dynamite Offy camshafts of guru Smith. So, revamped for a fourth time, and newly christened the *Unverdorben Special*, old *98 Jr.* went back to work, then didn't do much until the 1956 night when the Grove was throwing one of its "All-Indy" extravaganzas and Tony Bettenhausen and Jimmy Bryan were present palpating each other's jugulars, ready to get it on national champion-style. By contrast, on the buzzer of the now-ancient *Unverdorben* was little Charlie Musselman, a P-A regional and sometime-chauffeur of Sam Traylor iron whom Sam had gotten mad at and laid off. Bringing to violent life those Clay Smith cams and evoking the spirit of Rutt, carrot-top Charlie mounted a romping, stomping attack, and the *Unverdorben* won by leading Bettenhausen and Bryan every lap.

The bad karma that enveloped the *Nyquist Offy*, later the *Pfrommer Offy*, was ignored too. Originally

Sal Scarpitta in Los Angeles, 1995.
Neil Nissing

became parts of the *Elloy Cotton Chemical Association* sprinter, the "ECCA car," which for years was the scourge of Southwestern racing. Near the beginning of his dirt track highway career, Bobby Unser used it to annihilate a big fakeroo IMCA race in Sedalia, Missouri, and the following year baby brother Al won the same race in the same car.

Salem, Winchester, and Dayton Speedways were out-of-the-ordinary battle theaters whose paved and

another over-east sprinter, with parallel torsion bars front and rear, it got hauled west to the Midwestern slants in 1954. Sinister Salem struck again when the *Nyquist* cleared the walls and broke its spine in the same long fall to the ground that set fire to a cornfield and terminated Wally Campbell's days.

Less than a year afterward, following a major makeover by Hiram Hillegass, who laid on a new chassis, four-wheel disc brakes, and a bent sprint front, the *Nyquist* appeared at Langhorne for a pair of

3-A features. Winning the first, in the second it duplicated its Salem effort by crashing and launching from another track. Erasing Mike Nazaruk, it rearranged a quarter-mile of Bucks County property before ending its flips.

So the *Nyquist* was a catastrophe and now had to disappear? Hardly. Before crashing, Mike had set 'Horne speed marks in it, and that was good enough to earn it yet another makeover and new lease on life. Jud Larson—at first admitting apprehension at strapping

Jack McGrath's well-equipped *Hinkle Special* Kurtis-Kraft was a winner at Syracuse and Milwaukee. *Walter Kelting, Scalzo collection*

Dirt track tyros often were their own mechanics. Leroy Neumayer, coffin nail dangling out of his mouth, fine-tunes his *Diz Wilson Special* prior to a Minnesota State Fair. His bud Bobby Spere assists. *Al Herman, Jake Bozony collection*

on the one that had gotten Iron Mike—used it to have his wonderful 1956 afternoon at Reading, when the *Nyquist* broke Reading's one-lap record and almost toppled Hinnershitz.

The *Nyquist* next passed to the stable of John Pfrommer, who had eyes for Bob Tattersall, the World War II prisoner-of-war inmate who was supposed to be the new Wally Campbell but wasn't: bad Bob dumped the *Nyquist*. But then the often-crashed rig received the great compliment of going to master Hinnershitz himself, who completed his long 1931–1960 career with it. Still not done, it got repainted, revamped, renamed the

Pendleton Builders, and went back to work in the dirt minor leagues for another decade or so.

The *98 Jr./Umberdorben* Kurtis-Kraft received its original retweaking out in L.A. at the lordly facility of Eddie Kuzma; the Sweikert was kind of a three-way collaboration between Bob, A. J. Watson, and the brain Hank Blum (who happened to stop by Watson's shop on his lunch hour and ended up helping Bob do the calculus to get the suspension numbers right); and the *Nyquist* was another L.A. product created by Barnie Christianson.

During 1951–1971 it was difficult getting right who built which cars because lots of the constructors

were unknown to everybody but the complete insiders. As an example, the automobile that set my sprint car styling tastes forever, the amazing *HOW Special*, was the work of unheralded Bob DeBisschop, and was the only sprinter DeBisschop ever turned out. Bob had an engineer's degree, so his technical smarts were superior to most, and he was also hip to good looks because his street rod had caused a sensation at the bellwether 1947 Oakland Car Show.

In 1955–1956 DeBisschop was working for Mari Hulman and her new husband, Elmer George, and that was when Bob created the *HOW*, which stood for

Hulman, Ober (an Indianapolis judge and powerful political pal of the Hulmans), and Walcott (for Roger Walcott, a family friend with his own champ car team).

Stubby little stretched midgets were pretty much dominating the sprint car landscape, and Bob was looking for smoother lines as well as a lower center of gravity. Splitting the hood line at the motor plate to get the shape he was seeking, Bob additionally managed the significant double miracle of lowering the cockpit seat some six inches yet avoiding having the driver smash his spinal cord and butt against the Halibrand quick-change.

During the 1950s many of the fastest sprinters were so small they looked like midgets; trim, buzzing, flyweight race cars, they put on choice, racing-for-racing's-sake duels high on many a dirt track lip. The *Nyquist Offy*, later the *Pfrommer Offy*, was perhaps the most unpredictable. Wally Campbell and Mike Nazaruk took their last rides in it, but it provided great transporation to Jud Larson and Tommy Hinnershitz. *Walt Imlay, Stew Reamer Collection*

"I ran out of brakes—'n' brains—and then I triggered it," joked a bruised and sore Roger McCluskey after taking this 1961 sprint car flopper at Indianapolis Raceway Park. The Indy 500 was two days later but, hurts and all, Roger competed anyway and somehow managed to get tangled up in yet another cruncher. His sprinter is the Bob DeBisschop beauty that raced and won through 10 fierce campaigns.
Bob Tronolone

The *HOW* was off-the-trailer fast with great steering recovery—it was next to impossible to spin out. While Offy-powered, it captured the Midwest championship of 1957, and it remained fast after Quin Epperly gave the *HOW's* rear suspension an update in 1960, and it acquired a V-8 Chevy in 1962. In 1963, when it was 7 years old and should have been in its dotage, DeBisschop's bomb came into its own. It got a new custodian/owner, Don Shepherd, and its USAC chauffeurs Johnny Rutherford and Bobby Unser put much of the muscle into 1960s' racing. Come 1965, when the car was entering its 10th campaign, it was in the middle of the fight for the season championship thanks to Shep and Bobby. DeBisschop came to Ascot Park's finale to watch. By then Bob had done turns of employment with A. J. Watson, made taxicab mills for Jack Zink, and at his engineer post at AiResearch was bootstrapping the turbocharged Offy project. After watching his old car catch an Ascot wall—Bobby and A. J. Foyt had an unscheduled meeting—Bob decided that dirt racing hadn't changed. Race cars still raced forever, still hammered walls, still got repaired, and continued on.

3

Eddie, Clint, Bob, and Jimmy

By the middle of the 1950s, almost everyone but Frank Kurtis was in agreement that while Kurtis-Kraft and its *Bellanger 99* had first been the way to go dirt champ car racing, now it was mandatory to go with Eddie Kuzma. Out of 1953–1958's 44 mile-track 100s, Kuzmas won 26. More striking still, just five Kuzmas were responsible for all the domination. They were the *Agajanian 98* of 1951, the *Agajanian 97* of 1952, the *Peter Schmidt* and the *Dean Van Lines* of 1953, and the *D-A Lubricants* of 1955.

Eddie's chariots started taking over in a big way at the inaugural Hoosier Hundred of 1953, when the *Dean Van Lines* and the *Peter Schmidt* almost dead-heated for first after both had gotten stacked-up two weeks earlier. The next year the *Dean* and *Schmidt* proceeded to run one-two at Phoenix, showing the Kuzma superiority on rough tracks.

Then in 1956 at Syracuse, the leading *D-A Lubricants* was run down on the back-straight by the *Schmidt* followed by the *Dean*, yielding the first 1-2-3 (Schmidt/Dean/D-A) Kuzma finish. Yet what everyone

4

Pick your style of shoe—block treads, diamonds, Goodyear Suburbanite retreads, etc.—the wrong set of rubber would cost you the race. Knobs such as these were the ticket over east and out in the IMCA Midwest. So long as the driver kept his hoof in it and the dirt churning, all was well; if he was timid, however, knobs fired him toward the wall. *Jake Bozony collection*

really cared most about was how a champ dirt car worked at Langhorne, and Langhorne was where Kuzma results spoke for themselves. For five of six 'Hornes, nothing but an Eddie car won.

The histories of the *Agajanian 98*, the *Agajanian 97*, the *Schmidt*, and the *D-A* can be briefly told. The *Agajanian 98* in 1951 smashed all qualifying marks on Indy's bricks, and on the dirt tracks beat the *Bellanger 99* at Milwaukee. In 1952 it won Indy, Detroit, and Denver. In 1956 it sat on Langhorne's pole, then raced on under different names for another dozen years. The *Agajanian 97* in 1952 won Milwaukee, DuQuoin, and the AAA's seasonal championship. In 1953 and 1954 it won Milwaukee again. In 1956 it won Langhorne. And in 1959 it won Springfield. The *Schmidt* won Milwaukee in 1955, and in 1958 it won Langhorne and the Hoosier Hundred. In 1960 it got its second Langhorne scalp. The *D-A* in 1957 captured Langhorne's "race of the century," setting an impossible speed record dancing around the 'Horne for 100 miles in 59 minutes and 53.74 seconds, including the minute it lost sitting in the pits while its crew scrambled to change a shredded right rear. In 1958 it won DuQuoin, Syracuse, and Sacramento. In 1959 it won Sacramento. In 1961–1962 it won Springfield.

Racing being racing, some grief had to go along with all that Kuzma glory.

At the heat-stricken 1953 Indy, the *Agajanian 98* was such a handful it wore out its original driver, two relief drivers, and at last broke a front axle and popped the wall. Back at the Brickyard in 1955 it was sponsored by Hollywood cowboy Hoot Gibson and named the *Aristo Blue Special* after Gibson's chinchilla ranch. Three miles per hour off the qualifying pace and all set to miss the 500, the assigned driver threw up his hands in futility, told his mechanics to do something, and went off to play gin rummy. For a placebo, all the mechanics could think to do was apply a wax job, and the driver, impressed with all the glitter, proceeded to put it in the show. But in the 500 the front axle snapped again and the *Aristo Blue* flipped over and was the crucial player in Vukovich's 57th lap spill.

The *Agajanian 97*, in the lead at the 1954 DuQuoin, bumped into a laggard Kurtis-Kraft that was circulating without brakes and sent the Kurtis into the DuQuoin signaling pits, where it hit and killed 97 celebrity mechanic Clay Smith. In a 1958 crash the car's own driver got carried away.

Frank Kurtis. Through 1951–1953 his Kurtis-Krafts went on a rip of dirt track miles, winning 10 of 12 meets in 1951, 7 of 9 in 1952, then going 9 for 10 in 1953. But for the rest of the 1950s, it was a Kuzma parade. There were just three more Kurtis scores, including the last one ever, a thundering upset at the 1959 Langhorne. *Bob Tronolone*

The original *Springfield Welding Special* came out of the Kurtis-Kraft shops in 1952. Ten years, many remakes, three paint and name changes, nine drivers, and one engine swap (from Offy to Chevy) later, the antique was still slowly patrolling the mile tracks. The Los Angeles journeyman Colby Scroggin gets lapped at Sacramento by Don Branson and a typically rim-riding Bobby Marshman. *Bob Tronolone*

The last championship victory ever for a Kurtis-Kraft went to this *Vargo Engineering* at Langhorne. Hoo-doo wagon! It was dirt racing's answer to the Porsche Spyder of Jimmy Dean, or even to the Graf and Sift assassination limo of Archduke Ferdinand in which 10 people were reportedly killed over the next nine years. It began life as the *Belond Equa-Flo* and at Detroit in 1953 ripped to pieces Johnnie Parsons' palms. Then it got lost on a railroad siding. Then Sam Traylor owned it, and Al Keller took a strange ride in it at Atlanta in 1956. By 1959 it was the *Vargo*. That spring, jumping out of paved Trenton, it claimed its first driver, Dick Linder; that same summer at Williams Grove—right after Van Johnson had made it a Langhorne champion—it got its second, Van himself. At Langhorne 1962, here, it wore out its assigned driver, a relief driver, and then pounced fatally on a second relief driver, Hugh Randall. *Bruce Craig*

Near the top of the list of the really honkin' Offy midgets was the *Hollywood Spring and Axle*, an ever-potent antique raced by Parnelli Jones and prepped by the redoubtable Johnnie Pouelsen. *Bob Tronolone*

The *Konstant Hot* sprinter was called "the first modern sprint car" because of its four-bar suspension. It damn near made everything else obsolete. Constructed by Jud Phillips in 1962, in five USAC tournaments it won three national titles; put Roger McCluskey on Broadway again after he badly fractured an arm in a Meskowski iron; and was so potent it almost let sprinter novice (but go-kart icon) Mickey Rupp realize his goal of pinning a defeat on A. J. Foyt. This is the car when Mutt Anderson owned it in 1966, McCluskey up, making an Ascot inside move on A. J. Foyt and Hal Minyard. *Dwight Vaccaro*

As for the *Schmidt* and the *D-A*, neither one ever destroyed anyone, but between themselves they succeeded in getting upside-down three different times at Langhorne, all courtesy of the same driver.

Impressive as those Kuzmas were, though, they were minor players compared to the *Dean Van Lines Special*, champion of 17 100-milers, including eight consecutive match wins. In such a class of its own was the *Dean*—other drivers would have loved visiting the rough parts of mile tracks where the *Dean* went, but could not—that rival cars were barely missing a crash a lap keeping up—or not keeping up. A lot of its greatness was due to the *Dean Van Lines* itself. A lot of it was because of its two drivers, Bob Sweikert and Jimmy Bryan. And a lot of it was courtesy of its holy terror of a chief mechanic, Clint Brawner—hardliner, roarer, inspired racing strategist, sly deceiver, and the only

chief so outspoken he was barred from setting foot inside the Kuzma compound.

Eddie Kuzma's in southern L.A. was home to racing's hottest tin benders and fabricators, including Fat Boy Ewing, Joe Fuchishima, Roger Beck, and Don Edmunds. All of them were somewhat in awe of Eddie, who throughout 1951–1971 was dirt racing's foremost race car-building loner/eccentric. However, nobody had anything to fear from Eddie so long as their work got done on time.

Kuzma's was always busy. Typically, a morning kicked off with Eddie telling each associate his particular assignment, then leaving him alone to complete it. Conversation was discouraged—supposedly it was why Eddie always had the radio roaring away. A labor break of sorts occurred at mid-morning when Eddie tersely called, "Coffee." Everybody followed the boss to where

The Indy 500–winning *Agajanian Special* was the Eddie car that kicked off the Kuzma dominance. *Scalzo collection*

the pot was brewing, watched Eddie throw back a scalding cup's worth and did the same themselves, then beat it back to work again until lunch. Then there was the afternoon charge.

Getting to construct, rehabilitate, and repair race cars right alongside Eddie was judged the highest honor going and only L.A.'s finest talents ever got to, usually. But one time chatterbox Eddie Sachs somehow slipped past security and landed a Kuzma gig. Sachs knew nothing about race cars except how to drive them very fast, and after disemboweling a fuel tank without first draining the contents, he suddenly had Kuzma's in a

flood of raw alcohol with deep puddles forming beneath a lighted water heater. The fallout was that the entire shop had to be temporarily evacuated, and Sachs found himself joining the shit-listed Clint Brawner on Eddie's persona non grata list.

Sachs later managed to get back on Eddie's good side, and his Kuzma visiting privileges were restored, but Clint never made it. What, exactly, had provoked the feud between the great car builder and the great chief mechanic was never known for sure, but it was almost comic: through the 1950s Dean Van Lines faithfully purchased the Kuzma hardware, and Dean's

Seven long seasons after it had set time trial records at Indianapolis; six after it had won the Indy 500, Detroit, and Denver; three after it had been the bad actor in the big Brickyard back-straight mess that got Vookie; and two after it had set quick time at Langhorne, the *Agajanian 98* was looking less than first rate yet was still campaigning and in the middle of the action. This is the 1958 Sacramento 100. *Bob Tronolone*

superstar, Jimmy Bryan, was always Eddie's best advertisement. Yet on the rare occasion when they had to communicate at all, Clint and Eddie did it through intermediaries.

Well, nobody ever accused grizzled Clint of trying to win popularity contests, especially his drivers. All race drivers, to Clint, were sub-humans bent on tearing up his race cars. Bob Sweikert was one of many who fell under Clint's thumb. Jimmy Bryan may have been the making of the *Dean Van Lines Special*, but before Jimmy there had been Sweikert, who in 1953 was first to feel its potency. It was a strange tale. Bob had a good thing going with the *Dean*, but then he pulled the usual Sweikert screw-up and lost the ride. And after spending a frustrating 1954 and 1955 trying to correct the mistake and get back inside another Kuzma—and being on

the verge of doing so—in 1956 he instead committed his last screw-up and that was the end of him.

Bob was a dynamic devil with the outspokenness of a Foyt and possibly the talent: there are Sweikert enthusiasts who to this day claim Bob was the United States's greatest. Liking things to go his way, when they didn't, Bob's helmet might come off and be hurled the length of the pits. He was astute with racing's nuts and bolts side; mechanics working too slowly on his race cars knew what it was like to have tools taken out of their hands so that Bob could do a better and faster job himself.

He was the *Dean Special's* very first driver, at the 1953 Indy 500, and didn't do much. Chief mechanic Brawner hired a blizzard of unsuccessful replacements all summer until again going with Bob. Still they had

In addition to the *Agajanian 98*, there was the *Agajanian 97*, which over time evolved into the *Central Excavating*. Throughout the 1950s it was on the receiving end of handsome rides from the likes of George Amick, who won Langhorne, and Len Sutton, who scored firsts on dirt and pavement alike. Central Excavating was out of Cleveland, and the Ohio outfit's driving force was its rugged owner, Pete Salemi. One rainy day over at the Richmond Heights suburb, Pete was out on a digging job by himself when the earth gave way and he plunged to the bottom of a 15-foot-deep pit. Despite being up to his chest in mud, and with injuries that included a broken arm and hip, powerful Pete single-handedly extricated himself from the pit. Then he drag-crawled to his car, which he piloted six miles to the hospital to check in for emergency treatment, passing out upon arrival. *Bob Tronolone*

no success. But then Clint made an inspired change of gear ratio and Bob set quick time at Syracuse with a blinding lap record that stood for 21 years. Despite wrecking in the race, he and the *Dean* had found each other and two weeks later won the Hoosier Hundred.

Feeling his oats afterward, Bob ran a bluff on Clint, telling the chief that unless Dean Van Lines paid him a $15,000 retainer and also bought him a new sprint car, he was going elsewhere in 1954. Calling his bluff, Clint informed Bob that Jimmy Bryan was replacing him.

Losing the ride in the *Dean*, then, was Bob's big blunder, and the best he could do afterward was score a 1954 assignment with a trucking-parts kingpin whose three-year-old Kurtis 4000, the *Lutes Trucking Special*, had known better days. How really far behind a Kuzma it was came to Bob that May in Indy when in a field of 13 roadsters and 20 upright dirt cars, he and the *Lutes* lined up two rows behind Jimmy Bryan, Clint Brawner, and Bob's old *Dean*. In the 500 Bob and the *Lutes* came in an uninspiring 13th and Bryan and the *Dean* took second and almost upset Vukovich and the vaunted *Fuel Injection Special* roadster.

The *Dean*, the *Agajanian 97*, and the *Peter Schmidt* all made Bob's life miserable through the next three months and five races, causing him to develop a complex

Len Sutton was one of at least four drivers able to coax a victory out of the original *Agajanian 97* Kuzma. *Bob Tronolone*

An Indy roadster was not an effective weapon to throw at a Kuzma like the *Dean Van Lines*. Johnny Boyd, here, outqualified Dean demigod Jimmy Bryan at the 1957 Phoenix 100, but watched helplessly as Jimmy left him well behind in the 100. *Bob Tronolone*

about Kurtis handling vs. Kuzma handling. There was a big difference. As one old chief mechanic told me, developing rapport between a Kurtis-Kraft's chassis and the vehicle's ton or so of poundage during a 100-mile race on a ragged track was a futile drill that began with jacking up the rear end to an abnormal height so that a driver could steer with the 300 extra pounds of fuel in the rump. After 50 miles a lot of the alky had burned away, so for the next 30 miles or so the chassis felt halfway decent. But then for the last 20 or so the near-empty posterior would be squatting and the front end hiking up and again hard to turn.

More than the likes of Bettenhausen or Bryan did, Bob depended on a dirt car's front end staying planted. Abhorring all broadsliding (he once said he thought it

looked like a monkey committing an indecent act on a football) Bob preferring to sail into dirt corners so straight and deep that he wore out brakes throwing the hook and getting whoa-ed. Yet no *Lutes* chassis alterations he could think of delivered relief from the twisting, schizophrenic, Kurtis front suspension.

So, after he and the *Lutes* did poorly at Milwaukee, and were even slower at Du Quoin, Bob acted. Days before the next 100-miler at Syracuse, he looked up A. J. Watson, who'd earlier made him a sprint car, and for a favor asked A. J. to look over the *Lutes* and upgrade it. An everybody-helps-everybody-else atmosphere existed in 1951–1971, so A. J. graciously removed the front parallel Kurtis torsion bars and replaced them with a Kuzma-esque spring front. Bob repaid him by winning

Syracuse and in the process beating Watson's own runner-up *Bob Estes*.

Meanwhile, Jimmy, Clint, and the Dean Van Lines were themselves getting hooked to throw their four-year stranglehold on the championship trail. Winners of all four remaining 100s at Indianapolis, Sacramento, Phoenix, and Las Vegas, they became national titlists with twice as many points as the second-place Peter Schmidt outfit and nearly three times as many as Bob and the *Lutes*.

For 1955, Bob's Syracuse benefactor, A. J. Watson, became the new head of John Zink, and Bob, as Watson's new driver, won the Indy 500, the national cham-

pionship, and the Midwest sprint car crown—1955 was one miraculous year for Sweikert. Also, even though he never got to race it himself, Bob at last satisfied his ambition to have his own Kuzma by using some of his prize loot from the 500 to purchase the *Agajanian 97* (later sold to Bowes Seal Fast and George Bignotti). But by year's end Bob got teed off at the father and son Zinks for some reason and quit them to go with D-A Lubricants for 1956 and race D-A's Kuzma.

This proved to be yet another huge Sweikert screw-up, because Bob had squandered the chance to race the first of the new Watson roadsters, which were to win six Indy 500s. But the worst and final error was to come.

Under the custody of Eddie Sachs and Jim Hurtubise, the *Peter Schmidt Kuzma* won two Langhorne 100s. *Bob Tronolone*

Johnny Thomson and the *D-A Lubricants* Kuzma. Langhorne icons of 1957, in 1958 they won Springfield, DuQuoin, Syracuse, and Sacramento. *Bob Tronolone*

That June, at the Father's Day sprint car show at Salem, Bob, while under surprise attack from Smokey Elisian, locked up his sprinter's front brakes and vaulted himself out of the race track and into history.

The end of Sweikert was almost the end of serious mile-track competition for Jimmy, Clint, and the *Dean Van Lines.* They'd won five of 10 miles in 1954, and six of seven in 1955. Now, in 1956, Bob was missing, Tony Bettenhausen and Johnny Thomson were erratic, and only the fast but flaky Jud Larson was there to occasionally get in the their way. Yawning to themselves, the trio won Springfield and the Hoosier Hundred, got the shaft at Phoenix, and if the *Dean* hadn't run dry of fuel would have taken their third straight Langhorne.

They might well have won Atlanta, too, except for getting tangled up in another typical racing adventure. Clint and a sprint car personality and roadie named Tiger Valenta were on the road with the *Dean*, and Clint was tearing up the blacktop when he lost it in some Kentucky hills near Frankfort. Pickup truck, trailer, *Dean Van Lines*, and Clint and Tiger all went crashing to the bottom of a gully. It took time to salvage everything, so Clint and Tiger went searching for shelter to hole up for the night. By outlandish coincidence, Clint had distant cousins in the neighborhood. That evening everyone got bombed and some of the female cousins and Tiger started playing grab-ass in the swimming pool—it was a disaster—and Clint and Tiger got thrown out. Having already missed Atlanta, it now seemed like the smashed-up *Dean* might miss the next show at Springfield too, because after Clint had hauled ass to L.A., Eddie Kuzma claimed to be too busy to do the repairs. Turning to Quin Epperly for relief, Clint had the *Dean* up and running again in time to win Springfield.

The *Dean* slowed a bit the next year. Or maybe the *Dean*, four hard years old, wasn't quite up to the new Walcott, Hopkins, and Bowes Specials from Lujie Lesovsky. Whatever, it won but two races, DuQuoin and the 1957 closer at Phoenix, where Jimmy Bryan outdid himself. After either getting crowded off the groove or just in his typical exuberance losing it, Jimmy left the track—he literally disappeared through a hole in the fence. And just when everyone thought they'd seen the last of the *Dean Van Lines* this time, Jimmy re-entered the race, bringing pieces of the fence with him.

The *Dean* passed on to other hands—A. J. Foyt made a debutante bow in it in 1958 and Al Unser did in 1965, at Sacramento, where Al's posterior got fried by the hot seat. The *Bellanger 99* had a great record, but the *Dean Van Lines* won three Phoenix 100s, two Springfields, two Langhornes, two DuQuoins, two Sacramentos, and four Hoosier Hundreds.

Courtesy of Johnny Thomson, five mile-track 100 scores had been racked up by the *D-A Lubricants* when Jim Hurtubise pulled wheelhouse duty in 1959. Through the following three tournaments, Herkie won three more. *Bob Tronolone*

Abram and Anthony Joseph

Some critics have charged that if Eddie Kuzma had only constructed his disappointing Indianapolis roadsters the same way he did the *Agajanian 98* and *97*, the *Peter Schmidt*, the *Dean Van Lines*, and the *D-A Lubricants*, then maybe the 500 wouldn't have been the Watson parade it was. Eddie's unsatisfactory Offy roadsters varied wildly from uprights to laydowns; it was as if there wasn't a package that satisfied Eddie. Yet once his Kuzma dirt cars had taken off and began dominating, he kept the same chassis formula and suspension combination season in and season out. Of course, the "secret" of A. J. Watson's unstoppable roadsters was that they, too, remained monolithically identical, just like the handful of dirt champ cars A. J. created for John Zink and *Leader Card*. All but one of these duplicated the dimensions of a Watson roadster, minus the chassis offset, and with the Offy exhaust out the right side instead of the left.

The exception was the very first John Zink, a bent-springer that A. J. constructed in year one of his bittersweet 1955–1958 association with the Zinks. Active through at least eight campaigns, its cockpit was filled with Indianapolis winners, national champions, a goofball icon, and one very desperate character. It won the Hoosier Hundred, Syracuse, Sacramento, DuQuoin, Atlanta, got bent at Langhorne, and was wrecked at Springfield. In 1961 I saw it get massacred in another Phoenix flip and was sure that really was the end of it; but no, with stock-block steroids it came back to get in still another stupid wreck on Milwaukee's pavement.

By 1959 A. J. was beginning his association with *Leader Card* and his focus was Indianapolis and an expanding clientele of roadster customers. Cutting-edge dirt track technology had been taken over by Wally Meskowski, who in a 1958 experiment had mated the standard Indy 500 suspension of four torsion bars going across the front and rear to a Hoover Motor Express. The experiment was a success. "If it works, plagiarize it," being the universal rule of race car constructors, A. J.'s *Leader Card 5* of 1959 was such a design.

Dean Van Lines' juggernaut Bob Sweikert/Jimmy Bryan/A. J. Foyt-mobile of 1952–1959 was at last replaced by this 1960 Kuzma, here being wrung out at Sacramento by Mario Andretti. The dramatic likes of Eddie Sachs, Troy Ruttman, and Chuck Hulse also exercised the *Dean* at one mile or another. *Bob Tronolone*

Champion of DuQuoin and the Hoosier Hundred in 1959, in 1960 at Langhorne the *Leader Card 5* acquired the notoriety of being the automobile that did the seemingly impossible: it took the life of Jimmy Bryan. To some sensibilities, that foul deed should have earned it banishment from racing forever. Dirt track racing, however, had no space for such wasteful sentimentality. Repaired and repainted, the *Leader Card 5* went on to win the 1960 Hoosier Hundred, the 1962 Langhorne, the 1965 DuQuoin and Sacramento, and the 1966 Springfield as well as establishing a tour de force time trial mark at Sacramento.

In the great *Leader Card* season of 1962, A. J. briefly interrupted his roadster-making labors to create the *Leader Card 3*. Through the seasons it won the Hoosier Hundred, Syracuse, Sacramento, Phoenix, and Springfield. Springfield also was where, in 1968, it went sailing out of the fairgrounds to crash-land in many pieces with no injury to its driver. Patched up again, the *Leader Card 3* went on racing in different liveries for another six tournaments.

With A. J.'s fingerprints all over three outstanding dirt champ cars, and naturally the 23 Watson roadsters,

A. J. Watson didn't limit himself to merely constructing the Offy roadsters that threw a stranglehold on the Indy 500. His sprints and mile-track hardware extended the Watson pedigree to dirt as well. *Bob Tronolone*

Many of the regular members of the familiar *Leader Card* cast caught on the starting line of the 1959 Sacramento 100: LeRoy Payne (wearing shades), boss Bob Wilke, a frowning Chickie Hirashima, and Rodger Ward, who won the race. Rodger's *No. 5* shows that Watson—just out of photo on the right—was experimenting with an unusual Indy 500–type, left-side Meyer-Drake exhaust pipe. *Bob Tronolone*

it may come as a surprise to hear that A. J.'s *1959 Columbus Auto Supply*, an Offy sprint car, piled up a record equaling or even exceeding any of the Watson long-wheelbase wagons. The *Columbus* also led to the landmark matching of Abram Joseph Watson with Anthony Joseph Foyt. Foyt, still something of a beginner in 1959, was the *Columbus'* very first driver, but when his second places began tapering off to sevenths and eighths he fell afoul of the untender mercies of the vehicle's head mechanic and got fired. Firing A. J., though, didn't improve the performance of the *Columbus Auto Parts*, and the team went under.

Watson reacquired the *Columbus*, renamed it the *Dart Kart*, and Foyt's driving privileges were restored. For

all of that hairy 1960 campaign it was A. J. and the *Dart Kart* against Parnelli Jones and Herk Hurtubise in their hot rod stock blocks. The *Dart Kart's* little 220 Offy was antediluvian: Louie Meyer and Dale Drake weren't even selling 220s anymore, and, being 100 cubes smaller and 30 horses weaker than the 321-inch Chevs, the Dart Kart should have been no match. But Foyt behaved like it was—at one of those "Twin 50" spectacles at the 'Horne he demonstrated that the Watson 220 had so much in reserve he was able to jack up the pace on the Chevys by two miles per hour. Anyone who got to see any of those A. J./Parnelli/Herk world wars is blessed.

Parnelli and Herk came out roaring anew in 1961. Parnelli had his same raging 321 as well as a killer 351.

Herkie wasn't hurting for horses either. A. J. was in good shape, though. As a reward for his winning them the 1960 national dirt champ car title, A. J.'s angels at Bowes Seal Fast had bought him the *Dart Kart*. But for A. J. the really welcome news was that George Bignotti, who owned half of the Bowes team, and who in many minds had replaced Clint Brawner as racing's most vaunted mechanic, was going to personally interest

himself in the vehicle's maintenance. Like A. J., George was just coming into his prime.

Bignotti had his special sources, and they were blue chip. Ed Winfield had taken a shine to George, and was busy grinding trick camshafts for the 220 to go along with the special pistons and connecting rods George was tooling up on his own. George had a strong working knowledge of nitromethane and other dangerous

With help from a huffing and puffing Chickie Hirashima on the left rear, A. J. Watson pushes Rodger Ward's *Leader Card 2* to its outside front row starting hole at the 1961 Sacramento 100. Rodger won again. *Bob Tronolone*

power additives, and his selections of what gears A. J. should pull were inspired. A. J. ran Parnelli, Herk, and their bow ties ragged!

Terre Haute was the favored Offy vs. Chev combat shrine, and Foyt pundits maintain that the Action Track was where A. J. always extended himself to the absolute peak of his talents—whether in midgets or sprint cars. This one monster main event in summer of 1961 saw Herk lead, then Parnelli, and then the two together took over the bottom groove leaving A. J. nowhere to go but upstairs. Before A. J. well and truly ventilated Bignotti's best 220, he had gotten ahead of both Chevys. Not long afterward at Williams Grove he hammered them all over again for 50 laps, this time without blowing.

The *Columbus Auto Supply/Dart Kart/Bowes Seal Fast* sprinter was Foyt's baby. Not only did he never pile it up or get it on top of him, he only spun it out one time, at the Action Track, and he became so irritated afterward that he hurt his big toe giving it a kick in the tail. It got sold in 1962. The last show I ever heard of it winning was one of those California Racing Association extravaganzas on the Phoenix mile.

Throughout 1960–1961, A. J. Foyt in his Offy-powered *Bowes Seal Fast* Watson sprinter went after the big, dominant bow tie V-8s of Parnelli and Herk. He fought the big Chevys to the bitter end even if it occasionally meant "putting a window" in the overstressed 220 block. *Bob Tronolone*

Bob Sweikert and Jud Larson—Mr. Keep-It-Straight and Mr. Broadslide—both raced the *John Zink*, the trusty Watson that in four campaigns won Atlanta, Syracuse, DuQuoin, Sacramento, and the Hoosier Hundred. *Bob Tronolone*

Tony Bettenhausen was said to bring an extra 100 horsepower to everything he touched; he exercised his chariots to the limit whether they liked it or not. The *John Zink*, Tony's 1958 ride, presumably is letting out a groan of anticipation as the Panzer saddles up. *Bob Tronolone*

Johnny Rutherford and the 1965 *Leader Card Moog-St. Louis*, a Syracuse-Springfield-Hoosier Hundred-Sacramento-Phoenix-winning Watson. *Bob Tronolone*

Lujie's Duplicates

Most of the 200-odd champ dirt cars, sprints, and midgets constructed through 1951–1971 didn't live up to their builders' expectations and were, for one reason or another, failures. They never won any races, and never earned back the money that car owners and race teams had paid for them. This was yet another reason why teams fortunate enough to field a winner kept on racing the same car year after year instead of going with anything new. And why the rule was, if a design works, steal it.

Yet building an exact copy of some other builder's successful car was no sure thing either. Lujie Lesovsky discovered this in 1961 when Mari Hulman George

asked him to duplicate the DeBisschop *HOW* sprinter and Lujie agreed to try. But Lujie's subsequent *American Platformate* did only so-so, even after A. J. Foyt purchased it and campaigned it as the *Traco Engineering*. This was just one of Lujie's dirt car disappointments.

As the constructor of the unstoppable *Bellanger 99*, the Tony Bettenhausen rocket that was 1951–1971's first great champ car, Lujie's reputation for a time was secure. The *Bellanger 99* was strictly an emergency-ward job, brought to Lujie and his then-partner Quin Epperly in desperation—-and in half a dozen or so pieces—after going tree-whacking in a 1950 spill at Sacramento. Starting life as a radically stretched Kurtis-Kraft midget, it had to be totally wrecked before being

108

Lujie Lesovsky champ dirt winners including the *Walcott*, the *Bowes Seal Fast*, and the *Hopkins*, here, champion of Phoenix and Atlanta. *Bob Tronolone*

put right. In 1951 the *99* proceeded to win nine races, including Indy (with ill-fated Lee Wallard), where it was the first automobile to cover the 500 miles in less than four hours.

The *Blue Crown*, a 1951 Lesovsky that raced under at least 10 different names and liveries through the next 16 seasons, and did some extremely serious and effective warring, was another outstanding Lujie car. But Lujie's 1952 clone of the *Bellanger 99* was a flop, and for three years he was more successful repairing and recycling wrecked Kuzmas and Kurtis-Krafts than he was at creating his own Lesovskys.

In 1955, however, Lujie turned out the Kuzma-influenced *Walcott Fuel Injection* and the *Hopkins*. It took almost two season to get both of them going, and at first nobody could overcome the hopping-up-and-down front wheels that were a diabolical Lujie trademark. But by the summer of 1957 the *Walcott* and the *Hopkins* were the twin talks of dirt: chief mechanic Herb Porter and Rodger Ward had won Springfield and Sacramento in runaways, and Jack Beckley and George Amick took Atlanta and, earlier, the 1956 Phoenix. George Bignotti became so enamored that in 1958 he had Lujie drum up the *Bowes Seal Fast*, a replica Walcott that was so close to the original it even had a bend

Bobby Grim, outside, in the *Bowes Seal Fast* Lesovsky; Tony Bettenhausen, inside, in the *Hopkins* Kuzma.
Bob Tronolone

Phoenix and Atlanta champion George Amick joined Jim Packard, Rodger Ward, and Jud Larson as winners for the Lesovsky marque. *Bob Tronolone*

in its engine bay to accommodate Herb Porter's occasional supercharger, even though George had no plans to run a huffer.

George would mature into 1951–1971's genius chief mechanic, but at this point he was still finding his way. Not always fruitfully, he experimented a lot with the *Bowes Seal Fast*. Adding struts to cure the chronic Lesovsky front wheel hop was a success, but George's

venture into improved exhaust scavenging became an expensive disaster for himself and a painful one for *Bowes* driver Johnny Boyd. It happened at Langhorne in 1958. With its molten exhaust pipe atypically running underneath the chassis instead of along the side, the *Bowes* was actually setting fire to Langhorne's black sludge surface every time its Offy backfired. In addition, George had the *Bowes* burning an explosive

Seldom seen out of its Southern California bailiwick, where it dominated California Racing Association melees season after season, the Morales Offy *Tamale Wagon* made a rare, unsuccessful visit to Indianapolis Raceway Park in 1961. *Bob Tronolone*

methanol-nitro blend. Finally, thanks to bumpy old Langhorne, the fuel tank of the *Bowes* was pounding against the Halibrand center section so fiercely that a hole the size of a quarter opened up.

The result was a real chain-reaction holocaust. Everything detonated, and after Boyd bailed out with second- and third-degree burns, the *Bowes* went on flaming—it had magnesium components—until it seemed nothing was left. Sufficient Lesovsky merchandise was left, though, for Bignotti to work some restoration magic and haul it to Phoenix that November, where the *Bowes* earned him his very first victory as

champ car chief. But it had taken one of Jud Larson's deluxe chauffeuring jobs to do it, and for the rest of 1951–1971 no Lesovsky won on dirt again, except for the clapped-out old *Blue Crown* at Springfield in 1960 with ultrainspired Jim Packard in its bucket.

Four-Bar Wally

Mario Andretti, one of the crucial participants in the compelling sprint car series of 1966, once remarked that all of that magic but costly year the spectators were watching the wrong people. Instead of watching him dueling his brains out with Bobby Unser, Mario

suggested that everyone should have been digging Don Shepherd, Bobby's car owner, arguing with and shooting death looks at Mario's equally assertive owner, Wally Meskowski—Shep being fiercely protective of his boy Bobby, and Wally standing up for his boy Mario. Actually, more people were watching Shep and Wally than Mario imagined. Even rival chiefs stood back in

appreciation of the high-energy hysterics as Shep and Wally flailed their arms, brandished their fists (and wheel hammers), and called down a chilling series of curses on each other besides issuing a rolling barrage of threats at enemy cars.

Even so, it's unfortunate for Wally's posterity that he got so swallowed up in his role of archetype angry

Wally Meskowski and the *Competition Engineering* of 1961. Hot dog chauffeurs such as Bobby Marshman, Bobby Marvin, Eddie Sachs, and Herk all raced it, yet by some fluke it never won a feature race. *Bob Tronolone*

A. J. debuted the *Sheraton-Thompson Meskowski 2* at the 1963 Sacramento 100 (opposite). A year later at the same race (left), it had become champion of all mile-track racing. *Bob Tronolone*

Having spent his merry mile-track life almost exclusively belted inside the Watson and Lesovsky marques, Jud Larson, in 1965, at last got to wring out a Meskowski, the *Federal Engineering*. Naturally he ran it just as crossways as he had everything else. *Bob Tronolone*

sprint car owner that many of his other accomplishments were largely forgotten. For one thing, he was a talent-spotter of high order: years before George Bignotti had "found" A. J. Foyt, for instance, Wally had novice A. J. at the wheel of his sprinters and dirt champ cars (the two also had their well-known disagreement at Indy Raceway Park in 1965). And even though Wally was a Hoosier Clem and therefore not as famous as the big guns on the left coast like Kurtis-Kraft, Kuzma, Watson, and Lesovsky, his car-construction expertise was exceptional as well, and, as previously noted, he was the first constructor to put a four-bar roadster suspension under a dirt car and make it work.

The term "four bar" entering the racing vocabulary wasn't a blessing for those of us who previously could go to races and enjoy them without knowing much about race cars. From their Meyer-Drake Offenhausers to their solid-beam axles to their ribbed Firestone fronts and block-tread rears, every champ dirt car, sprinter, and midget looked and seemed to behave almost the same. But after the four-bar hit, it became such an advantage that to know what was going on, you had to know which car was a four-bar and which wasn't.

One driver told me that comparing an old bent-spring suspension to a new four-bar was like comparing being in a storm at sea in a rowboat or a luxury liner. Four-bar delivered a finesse feel; negotiating even a badly rutted corner, you could hang loose all the way. Wally was really on to something, and anyone lacking a four-bar was technologically challenged.

The Meskowski works were located in what was formerly Bob Sweikert's headquarters, across 16th Street from the White Front in Indianapolis. Either because he didn't have much room or was too busy out on the circuit barnstorming his sprint cars, Wally turned out few cars, roughly half a dozen. This was mostly during the 1960s, a decade when Watson won 11 races, Kuzmas of the four-bar design won 6, and Grant King's cars won 8. Wally's won a staggering 26!

His customer teams included Bill Forbes, Mari Hulman George, Lindsey Hopkins, and, conspicuously, Bowes Seal Fast and Sheraton-Thompson. Those last two were George Bignotti/A. J. Foyt squads, and Bignotti used his favorite fabricator, Eddie Kuzma, to fine-tune and implement radius rod subtleties unknown to other Meskowskis. As if repaying Wally for other career favors, A. J. was responsible for 23 of the Wally wins. A. J. won four times with the *1960 Bowes Seal Fast*, six times with the *1961 Sheraton-Thompson*, and a resounding nine times with the *1963 Sheraton-Thompson*, which swept all five mile-meets in 1964 then raced on for 14 additional years.

Chief mechanic Herb Porter, pilot Lloyd Ruby, and the fast but fickle *Racing Associates* stovebolt that Herb called "the Little Red Rooster." It had a huge, destructive hunger for rocker arms. *Bob Tronolone*

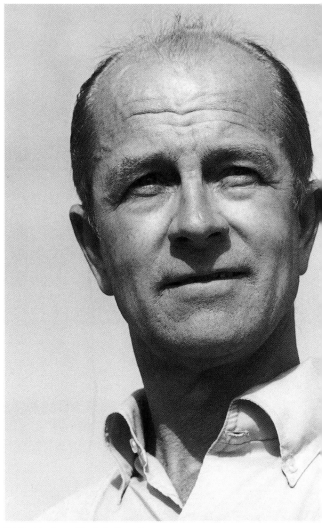

Wally Meskowski. *Bob Tronolone*

Looks That Kill

Critiquing the contours of a Wally Meskowski sprint car—possibly it was the one exercised by Bobby Marshman during Bobby's rim-ride assault of Terre Haute—designer Larry Shinoda complained, jokingly, that it looked "a little Polish." No one in racing was on the receiving end of more shopworn ancestral jokes than Nisei Larry, but he wasn't really deriding Wally's forebears (who came from Lithuania anyway). Instead, Larry was observing that Wally had committed the high crime of getting his styling off and had given the sprinter a swollen midsection.

Anyone who ever suggested that dirt track cars were primitive lumps designed solely to chew up the sod like tractors, surely had never encountered beauty fanatics like Dick Troutman, Jack Sutton, Hank Henry, Bob Pankratz,

or Fat Boy Ewing. Fastidious tin beaters all—and even though they realized that their handiwork was one day probably going to get clobbered in an accident—they went to often ludicrous lengths making graceful hoods, spillover bodies, aluminum flanks and underbellies, and whatever else was their chosen specialty. Fat Boy's obsession was grilles and noses. Ewing, who near the end got goofy and went off to live alone inside his decrepit Econoline van, once took a nose-building assignment from Gordon Schroeder, the power-steering titan. Following hundreds of distraught hours knowing that he wasn't

getting the nose right (even though Gordon was perfectly satisfied), Fat Boy completed his work. Then one midnight Gordon's telephone rang. It was Fat Boy, still distraught. He couldn't sleep from agonizing about the nose, so would Gordon allow him to trash it if he made Gordon a new one at no extra cost? Gordon said sure, and Fat Boy destroyed the nose with pleasure. Afterward he hung up the remains to curse and glare at while shaping Gordon a nose that pleased him.

Hank Henry was yet another of L.A.'s natural craftsmen and primitives who owned no special tools

Evergreen dirt tracker and chief mechanic Buster Warke—with his crusty pipe—chats with Herk about the *Sterling Plumbing*, one of the two wailing stock-blocks that ran 220 Offys out of sprint car racing. *Bob Tronolone*

and did everything by hand. While working, he'd straddle an old crankshaft he'd fashioned into a seat, which doubled as an anvil. Primitive or not, Hank fabricated noses, tails, hoods, seats, exhaust pipe headers, and aluminum fuel tanks of such exacting levels of craftsmanship that Eddie Kuzma once offered him a job, the highest compliment imaginable. Hank, however, said no—he enjoyed being an independent. His labor delivered more creative satisfaction than financial reward and he wouldn't make sprint cars for just anyone. His great work was the Parnelli Jones *Fike Plumbing Special*.

Exactly like Fat Boy, Hank had a critical eye for what looked good in the racing sense. When certain rival builders like A. J. Watson began producing sprinters without hood panels, thus exposing the engine, Hank was appalled—naked engines look ugly (Hank Henry cars came with panels *nobody* could remove). Aware of all fads and trends, he nevertheless stayed faithfully plugged into the past, and his cars reflected landmark builders he admired. His cockpit cowlings flared like those of Hiran Hillegass over east; Frank Kurtis was the other constructor whom Hank favored,

After 1960, sprint cars sacrificed their thin, classic lines—lines as symmetrical and pure as the old Meyer-Drake Offenhauser itself—and grew fatter and more ponderous to accommodate the Offy's dreaded gasket-engine foe, the Chev V-8. This is Parnelli Jones' *Fike Plumbing Special*, a Hank Henry chassis that, "fatness" aside, still looked great. *Harry Goode, Scalzo collection*

Artisan Hank Henry's first four-bar sprinter, the *J-Ram Chevy*, earned lanky, loose-as-a-goose Jimmy Oskie the seasonal championship of the California Racing Association in 1969, then four more in the 1970s. *Dwight Vaccaro*

and to some his cars looked like enlarged versions of Kurtis-Kraft midgets. A ruthless self-critic, Hank was never entirely satisfied with his perfectly proportioned cars. He complained that they looked like eggs moving down the track, meaning they were too rounded.

Hank was an unusual race car builder who also raced, and, really, he wasn't that good. A fiery smash-up on the Phoenix mile gave him serious burns over much of his body and especially his face and fingertips. Upon resuming work, he discovered that his mutilated fingers now lacked the dexterity to shape aluminum. But, as he optimistically noted, racing had gone to fiberglass anyway.

Occasionally, Hank did have his moments racing, and in a 1962 heat at Ascot he and Herk Hurtubise put on a wild display of crisscross dirt tracking that was long talked about and that Hank won. Ascot was also where Hank was killed: in 1968 he got tangled up with some rookies. It was a horrible wreck—one of Ascot's few out-of-the-ball-parkers—and witnessing it completely unnerved young Jan Opperman. Opp, who'd flown in by private plane and started just behind Hank, lapsed into shock while piloting over Bakersfield on the flying trip home, and he temporarily went blind.

Carrell Speedway winner Pappy Carter prepares to send a willing trophy damsel to paradise. Pappy's winning steed, a rail job that at the peak of its fame was named the *Black Deuce*, had as mighty a history as anything that ever raced. Eddie Kuzma shaped its hood and cowl, Bob Pankratz contributed the tail, and a greats gallery that included Rex Mays, Yo-Yo Ayulo, Mel Hanson, Billy Vukovich—Vookie!—plus Troy Ruttman—Rutt!—chauffeured it, Troy the most spectacularly. In 1951, beginning his association with Pankratz cars, Pappy Carter hauled out his checkbook to purchase the *Deuce*; soon afterward Pappy was upsetting Hinnershitz back at the Grove. Then Pappy installed Andy Linden at the wheel so that he, Pappy, could race that other great Pankratz, the *Cheesman* Offy. After deciding to conclude his arrangement with aggressive Andy and the *Cheesman*, Pappy sold the *Deuce* for $7,000—the same price he'd paid for it—to a racing medic from Connersville, southeast of Indianapolis. The doctor's driver was a TV antenna serviceman who reports say never got to race the M.D.'s purchase because he was electrocuted installing an antenna instead. Afterward, the now very old *Black Deuce* went to the East Coast, got butchered up, then restored, and disappeared into that vast elephant's graveyard of legendary race cars, the basement of Indy's Hall of Fame museum.
Raceway Photos, Scalzo collection

Opposite: Stubby wide tires changed dirt track racing. Look at all the security rubber Bobby Unser had to lean on in 1969. *Bob Tronolone*

Hank's ride that night had been one of the top chugs in the California Racing Association, a winner of many races, and a machine that was claimed to be what was left of an ancient single-tube Kurtis-Kraft linked to Johnny McDowell, Elmer George, Jerry Hoyt, Eddie Sachs, and Tony Bettenhausen. But this was a case where for once everyone was so pissed off about what a

race car had done to a good man that nobody tried restoring it. After being chopped into pieces, Hank's last ride was buried in a secret place where nobody could ever dig it up to try to race it again.

Still another "missing link" who tried bridging the gap between constructing cars and racing them was Bob Pankratz. But Bob, too, took a mauling from his racing.

He got into his first major spill before World War II and then experienced the big one from which he never quite recovered not long afterward.

Even before the spills, Bob was turning out gorgeous stuff seemingly better suited for the race car beauty contest than the dirt track. Pankratz sleds hugged the ground, displayed swoopy lines, employed the sort of Clyde Adams-like flat tails that Kuzma also favored, yet were extremely innovative with their low torsion bars and trademark Pankratz double radius rods. One notorious 1948 Pankratz midget, a looker as well as the kiss of death, nailed three different drivers. The first, a cinematically handsome Rex Mays protégé named Mel Hansen, absorbed paralyzing wounds after the Pankratz jumped on top of him. The second—we don't have to reveal his name—was a thief TV repairman and would-be racer who in 1952 ripped off the Pankratz and its trailer when he saw them parked on an L.A. street. He patiently cached the Pankratz for two years waiting for his theft to blow over, and then in 1954 at a Bay Cities Racing Association show in Sacramento didn't live through one lap's worth of time trials when the puppy jumped on top of him, too. A photo of the fatal flip made the AP wire, and everyone's knee-jerk reaction was "the dirty bastard yellow press is persecuting racing again!" but there was a brighter side. Someone identified the

For as long as anybody wanted to remember, the sound of dirt track racing was Offy, Offy, Offy, whether in midgets, sprints, or champ dirters. Compared to an Indy roadster, the standard mile-track Offy 255 sat backward in the engine bay, exhaust exiting to the right instead of the left. The Offy's thoroughbred but dated mile-track drone was at last silenced at 1960's end by Ford's screaming four-cammer, here wailing its heart out courtesy of George Bignotti and his best boy Jimmy Dilamarter. *Bob Tronolone*

Pankratz from the picture, and in time it was returned to its former owner, the trucking magnet and ex–Barney Oldfield associate Pat Clancy (himself an eccentric who had a six-wheel Indy car that was later converted to four by Fat Boy Ewing and campaigned by Diz Wilson). Pat in turn returned the Pankratz to its regular driver, the 110 Offy specialist Jimmie Davies. Better than a decade later, in 1966 at Chicago's Santa Fe Speedway, the same little car bit again, when the Pankratz stuck its throttle and plugged Jimmie into the wall. But the 17-year-old midget had by then won three straight USAC national championships and Jimmie had been working on a fourth.

Hands down the most luminous member of the Pankratz line was the *Cheesman* sprinter. Constructed in 1951, it raced in the Pacific Northwest and then was all over the Midwest, on the dirt tracks as well as the slants, winning the 1958 USAC title with Eddie Sachs up. Bill Cheesman died not long afterward, and Paul Leffler, a Wally Meskowski pupil just starting his own racing life as owner and chief mechanic, purchased the *Cheesman*. Despite being nearly 10 seasons old, it was arguably sprint racing's best-looking car, so Paul did his best to preserve its looks when he finally had to get rid of the outclassed Offy and open things up with a V-8 stove crammed inside the narrow Pankratz chassis. The makeover failed. In 1964, the *Cheesman* sailed over the

fence at New Bremen and crash-landed so hard it cracked into four pieces.

Paul salvaged what he could and rebuilt the chassis as *No. 16*. In 1966, just before the start of the June main event at Reading, Paul felt the hair on the back of his head standing up as he listened to his driver, none other than Jud Larson, uttering the standard Jud-ese about running it backward into the first corner. But Jud was past his prime and got hung up in the cushion instead, knocking out himself as well as Red Reigel in Johnny White's old car. And seemingly the *Cheesman*.

But not quite. Parts of it subsequently went on appearing on other cars. You can go to the loony bin trying to verify such stories, but five partners in West Virginia reputedly used bits off the *Cheesman* to construct a juggernaut that may have won 18 races on the West Virginia circuit.

It might appear that Bob Pankratz's reverence for beauty led him to create designs that jeopardized safety. But in 1951–1971 nobody expected race cars to be safe anyway. So maybe it's better to put it all down to the wisdom of Jack Kerouac. "Pretty chicks make graves," Jack wrote. So did pretty race cars.

No. 44

Still another important car that got recycled back to life in an unusual way was the old *Hoover Motor Express* that was responsible for A. J. Foyt's rookie launch at Springfield in 1957. A. J. promptly moved on to faster chugs, and in time the *Hoover* was taken to Diz Wilson's entrepôt in the south of Indiana so that Diz could scale it down from champ-car size to sprint-car size. Diz was great; when he wasn't busy racing or doing rehabs, he derived his income maintaining all the school buses for Indiana's Monroe County. The scenery at Diz's was equally great: a yardful of race cars and cast-off race cars—everything from Rangers to humongous 270 Offys—and many of them spray-painted a beautiful school bus yellow.

The revamped Hoover reemerged all glammed up as the *Werglund 44*. In 1963, ready for serious business, it arrived for the sprinter "Twin Fifties" at Langhorne—Langhorne's serious. And, indeed, at the morning drivers' meeting when Langhorne's major-domo Albert D. Gerber delivered his standard scary monologue about Langhorne being a place where a driver could righteously bust his ass if he was unwary, it seemed to some that it was directed toward Bobby Marvin. Bobby was the stocky and hard-faced blond

out of super-mods just picked by Andy Granatelli to race an unguided missile Novi at Indy, and at Langhorne the pilot of the *Werglund 44*. Those sharing the premonition weren't wrong, because Bobby and the *Werglund* were in for some big-ticket destruction. Bobby hooked and tore down a section of outer railing in Mike Nazaruk territory, then crashed terribly in a full burnout.

The Langhorne crowd fell silent, and one of the quietest was Sal Scarpitta. Not yet a race team owner, but already a racing captive after a boyhood's worth of Legion Ascot, he was in the grandstands of the second corner. "When something bad like that happens," Sal recalled recently, "I generally look to see what other peoples faces are like, or how they are gesturing. Because when you say that spectators come to watch wrecks, it's true. But more than just coming to watch wrecks, I think they're coming to get close to the wreck. There's a bonding that happens in the course of the wreck. You become bonded to the driver in the wreck—the bonding only lasting as long as the predicament lasts. And

the ones who become bonded really became a part of the race.

"So I went down on the track afterward and Bobby Marvin's cushion was there, and had been on fire. And I just pushed out as much of the horsehide and fabric as I could and quenched this smoldering mess. And I took it as well as some of the seat fasteners that were on some of the upholstery. And I made a painting of it, called *No. 44*, and it's in Italy at a museum in Turin now. I'm pleased with that, because in a small measure it continues to exert its presence. Not that I fancy myself important, but in my case I was able to pick something up, put some of my entity into it, and make my kind of music—music in this sense for people who fall. I just wanted to extend the life of this young guy."

The custodians of the *Werglund 44* were not so sentimental—they did what racers of 1951–1971 usually did. The burned-out *Werglund* was taken to Scats Anfuso and his P-A repair house for painting, grooming, and a new front end, then continued making its own music by racing on through another tough decade.

Bobby Marvin, here in the process of blowing sky high a Meskowski stock-block champ car during 1962 Sacramento 100 warm-ups, seemed to have it made going into 1963. He'd just been named USAC's "most improved driver" and Andy Granatelli was recruiting him to race one of the hell-fire Novis at Indy. Then Bobby committed the irrevocable error of visiting Langhorne instead. *Bob Tronolone*

Chapter 4

THE ELEVENTH COMMANDMENT AND "OOPS!"

There wasn't much money to be made covering racing for the trade papers circa 1951–1971, and the comic with the largest circulation, *National Speed Sport News*, was so tight that it wouldn't even reimburse postage. So the aspiring dirt track scribbler could flirt with starvation, and if that wasn't sufficiently risky he could take things up a notch and really expose his health to serious grief by defying the unspoken but sacrosanct 11th commandment of the dirt track gospel according to Jim Lunt, "Thou shalt write no evil of dirt track racing."

Good-hearted Jim, high priest of trade paper reporters, once advised in chilling detail what was in store for any rabble-rousing racing quill stupid enough to try to play Walter Winchell: "Cold stares, turned backs, friends becoming enemies, arguments and threats at banquets and other social functions . . . a punch in the mouth!" I believed and always followed Jim's commandment. Tempting as it is to say that he loved dirt track racing, tumors and all, it isn't true, because so far as Jim Lunt was concerned no tumors existed. Nobody worshipped dirt tracking more. Or was more fearful that one day it might be stopped. Jim had been on the beat forever, which was why he'd

never gotten over remembering the bloodbath at Imperial, the "kidnappings" at Forest Lawn, and all the antiracing poison flowing from the Hearst yellow press. All of that had happened in long-ago 1934, but Jim existed in full-blown paranoia and worked himself into a daily sweat worrying that fresh witch hunts were coming from racing's ever-implacable enemy, the swinish yellow-dog mainstream press, "who would like to see our sport curbed dramatically or even halted permanently."

Jim's trade paper readership—his congregation, actually—was huge, and his sermons preached vigilance. "Keep a stiff upper lip," fans were advised. "Guard your tongue at all times. Better to keep one's own counsel than to discuss accidents or injuries with a prejudiced nonracing public." Sometimes drivers got blasted for their unguarded tongues, too. Troy Ruttman—poor Rutt, forever taking gas for something—merely stated that he was quitting racing because he believed speeds were too high, and took this Jim Lunt hit: "We think it would be better if a driver, when he quits, admits he is scared or his reflexes are gone or old age is creeping in or whatever. Actually, he need only drop active participation and his followers

The 1960 Sacramento mile and another "oops!" As busted-up Eddie Sachs gets loaded into the back of the gore coach, his hurting *Dean Van Lines* Kuzma waits for somebody to come to its own rescue. *Bob Tronolone*

If you were a speak-no-evil chronicler of 1951–1971 racing, your most critical readership was typically here, in the pits of a champ car meet. Break the speak-no-evil commandment and you'd not see a pit pass again. *Bob Tronolone*

will understand and outside observers cannot criticize. We can recall numerous drivers who quit without any remarks that could hurt their beloved sport . . ."

Yet the daunting responsibility of making sure no harm came to racing rested strongest with Jim's colleague scribes, myself included. We were lectured solemnly, "Consider that opponents of auto racing also read your writings and pounce upon everything derogatory to the sport—*think that over.*"

Those were heavy orders to exist under, but I tried my best. Had I been a dirt track photographer, I'd have had it far worse. Right-thinking racing people of 1951–1971 were in agreement that anyone shooting pictures of a serious accident needed to have his film confiscated, his cameras smashed, and be subjected to a personal beating. So, when some lensman who didn't know the rules got caught snapping images of Joie James pinned in the wreckage of the

Bob Estes car on the San Jose mile in 1952, retribution was going to come down hard. Instead of taking his punishment, though, the photog ran for it. And just as the angry mob of pursuing fans, mechanics, and drivers closed in, the guy surprised everybody by jumping on top of a fire truck where he defended himself with a brandished ax. The promoter of the race finally rescued him.

There was a stringer for a racing trade paper whose byline was The Blind Reporter, and the poor devil literally was blind, as opposed to the rest of us word wizards, who, whenever something bad happened, were only mandated to be, per commandment 11.

Something bad happened—again—on the Phoenix mile, edition 1961.

This had been another one of those years when the Phoenix 100 was where the action was. The track surface was bombed-out, and down on the inside of one and two corners we'd been able to judge who fabricated the nicest set of belly pans—Kuzma? Watson? Meskowski?—because for the opening 49 miles all the cars were flashing them when they got up on two wheels. Parnelli Jones, Rodger Ward, and A. J. Foyt were making the pace. But then everyone stopped coming around and I couldn't tell what had stopped the race because the low-wattage P-A system didn't reach where I was standing.

I walked back around to the start and finish line and saw immediately that whatever had happened was indeed calamitous. Empty race cars were parked hurly-burly

The *Leader Card 2* looking typically Watson-clean and sanitary prior to the start of the 1961 Phoenix. But after one red flag and untold hundreds of crash landings on the standard Phoenix battleground, the same automobile—runner-up to the *Agajanian Willard Battery* Kuzma—looked ready for the Dumpster. *Bob Tronolone*

along the front straightaway and stewards, referees, drivers, and mechanics were milling all over the place in confusion. Far up the track, a couple hundred feet out of turn four, the desert sun was glaring off the yellow and red livery of Al Keller's *Konstant Hot Special*, which was parked on its wheels but all wrapped up in the outer chain-link fencing, badly wrecked. Medics had already removed Al, but there was blood, a lot of blood, splashed all over the broken windshield.

So we'd lost Keller—Sam Traylor's "Dirty Indian," a strong soldier/warrior of dirt who'd given up one of his thumbs to Langhorne, later been swindled out of victory in an Atlanta 100 when officials had let it run an extra mile, and been an uninvited instigator of the 1955 Vookie disaster at the Brickyard. Nobody said Al was gone, but the glistening windshield made the point.

Al had begun his Phoenix by breaking Rex Easton's three-year-old track record and winning pole with a lap time almost a second faster than anyone else. But in the race he lost the lead to Parnelli on the first lap, erratically caught a hole in turn one and dropped to ninth on the fourth, was lapped by Parnelli on the 42nd, then ate it completely on the 49th. I can still recall wondering at the time what in the world had been up with him. But I knew I wasn't going to do any morbid investigating of the "mishap," as fatalities were coded. Being overly inquisitive was in violation of Jim Lunt's commandment 11, maybe it even played into the hands of the enemy, and if I did write up something no trade rag would publish it anyway.

I took a walk farther down to turn four to study the thumping big hole that had neutralized Keller. A bulldozer was unsuccessfully trying to flatten it. Back at the pits, I checked out the various chugs for track damage and observed that the *Agajanian Willard Battery 98* had a fuel leak, the *Leader Card 2* had a flapping hood, the *Bell Lines Trucking* had deformed radius rods, the *Bowes Seal Fast* was coated with oil, and so on. There wasn't a completely sound car to be seen.

Standing among all the damaged iron equipment were the dazed and confused drivers, and I wondered what was in their heads—how many had slammed the same hole Al had, yet gotten away with it? Parnelli, the leader, had previously spun out and almost wrecked once. He was chain-smoking. Roger McCluskey, meantime, was visibly agitated because he'd purposely extended himself going a lap ahead of ever-dangerous Don Branson, who was known to fatigue during a 100's second-half. But at that very moment Don was back at

1961 Phoenix winner Parnelli. *Bob Tronolone*

Although suffering more mechanical failures than they should have, the combination of Parnelli and the *Agajanian Willard Battery* followed up their 1961 Phoenix score by taking the big money at the 1962 Hoosier Hundred. *Bob Tronolone*

"There's a hole in turn one—miss it!" was the succinct order that USAC stewards gave to the 18 starters at the 1961 Phoenix 100. Kind of a harsh send-off, but dirt drivers were like soldiers who were expected to race wherever their leaders sent them. Al Keller and Rodger Ward make up the first row; Parnelli Jones and Roger McCluskey the second. *Bob Tronolone*

his pit popping his "happy pills"—the red and blue bombers that were Branson's energy weapons. Once the race restarted with Don physically revived, Roger well knew, the old man's derring-do and rough-track prowess was going to sweep him, Roger, away.

Not helping to soothe anyone's mind was the standard tyrant crew of tubby stewards and aged referees with their USAC rulebooks, who were empowered to conduct the race. Nobody wanted to mess with those surly old crocks. Perhaps it violated commandment 11 to say so, but insider opinion held that whenever an ex-race driver, car owner, or even hanger-on grew old, fat, and crippled with senile dementia he was reindoctrinated into a dirt track steward or referee.

Phoenix's despots certainly lacked the humane touch. Their initial reaction to Keller's 49th lap plight had been to try to leave Al trapped and unattended in his crushed car for two green-flag laps so the race could reach 51 miles and be called complete. But this failed when all the outraged booing coming out of the main grandstands forced the red to be thrown. So now the surviving drivers and their ravaged sleds were getting the order to go back out and complete the remaining 51 miles on a ruined track that had already killed once.

But maybe they wouldn't have to. Working hard to have the rest of the proceedings cancelled and the standings of 49 miles posted as official, was, of all drivers,

Maybe there was a hole in number one at Phoenix, but a worse one lay hidden in turn four. Pole sitter Keller bingoed it on mile 49. And photog Bob Tronolone risked his own health snapping Al's brutalized *Konstant Hot. Bob Tronolone*

A. J. Foyt. I could see A. J. lobbying all the autocratic, beyond-it coot officials, then cajoling every driver one by one. I couldn't dope out why A. J. wanted Phoenix stopped while he was only running third; as dirt's premier rough-track driver, he'd undoubtedly win the whole shootin' match if things restarted. Yet there was A. J., playing Mr. Nice Guy, pleading that Phoenix must end before someone else got creamed, and pretty much having everyone agree with him until he got to Eddie Sachs.

A. J. and Eddie, it should be recalled, in May had fought one of the longest and most bitter duels in the annals of Offy roadster Indianapolis, and after their exchange of late pit stops A. J. had won and Eddie had lost. Whether Eddie was still upset about that, I don't know. Whether Eddie just didn't want A. J. to get his way, I don't know. Whether Eddie somehow had learned that at least part of the reason why A. J. wanted Phoenix curtailed was because A. J.'s own *Bowes Seal Fast Special* was getting ready to pop a piston and couldn't possibly travel an additional 51 miles, I don't know. Anyhow, far from agreeing with A. J. that Phoenix was lethal, Eddie smilingly declared that as far as he was concerned, Phoenix was in wonderful shape and that he couldn't wait for the restart!

The geezer stewards apparently had told A. J. that they'd call Phoenix only if *all* drivers wanted them to—and Eddie was kiboshing that. So A. J. ignited. Mr. Nice Guy turned into Mr. Ballistic. "Fuckin' Eddie!" A. J. screeched. Next came two even louder "Fuckin'

Parnelli Jones and his *Agajanian Willard Battery* (top), outside, beat off the likes of Eddie Sachs and Eddie's two-wheeling *Dean Van Lines* to win the restarted race, but Roger McCluskey in his *Bell Lines Trucking* (bottom) couldn't hold off Don Branson in the *Hopkins 5. Bob Tronolone*

Eddies!" Followed by a "Fuckin' Hee-brew!" Eddie, the foremost Jewish driver since Mauri Rose, for once kept quiet and went on smiling mockingly at A. J. It was superior entertainment that I never got to write about because of commandment 11.

There was an explosion of Offys, and Phoenix restarted. Physically and emotionally battered race drivers in disintegrating equipment were turned loose on an impossible track guaranteed to blur their vision as they fought it out averaging in the 90s, speeding into the glare of a setting sun—and without their cups of sake first, the way kamikazes set off in their Zeroes.

Horrible as it may sound, I thought the restart was one of the greatest things I'd ever witnessed. Now that I'm approaching the age of a USAC official, my new take on life is that you should live as long as you can. Yet 40 years ago at Phoenix there truly was something magnificent about seeing dirt track drivers following the old code of what somebody called "manly virtue and reckless bravado." Certainly the hazards and dangers of the dirt track were superior to the deadly boredom of the non-racing straight world; and another positive thing about dirt tracking dangers was that they kept the phonies away. Later I heard someone describe the situation in simpler terms.

One night in London, England, a wrinkled-up little stuntman named Pee Wee the Clown was on the top of tall and jam-packed Wembley Stadium watching Putt Mossman, a mad-hatter daredevil and Pee Wee's employer of the moment, prepare to ride a motorcycle off the Wembley roof and down a 300-foot tightrope into a tub of flaming gasoline. "I looked into Putt's eyes and could see that down deep he didn't want to go through with it," Pee Wee told me. "And then he went ahead and did. Just like that. Ever since, that's been my definition of guts. Real guts is going ahead and doing something that you don't really want to do."

Well, I don't know how many of those Phoenix lions truly wanted to do what they did, either. Parnelli discovered a hole in turn one, and almost but didn't overturn, then charged on to his first dirt champ car score. Roger McCluskey had all his fears confirmed when Don Branson, all revived with his go-go-go pharmaceuticals (they were actually harmless vitamins) got his lap back and more. A. J. did detonate a piston, which Eddie couldn't have been too upset about. And with 11 laps left, the remote control pilot of the *John Zink* succeeded in giving all of us a final fright by taking a long tumble across the back straight and massacring the former Bob Sweikert /Jud Larson ride. I ran over to see if this steering wheel–challenged lout was unharmed, and luckily he was, but the *John Zink* was downside-up and trashed.

Dennie Moore, the automobile's chief mechanic, had a confused expression, as if he was struggling to comprehend why the *John Zink's* driver—running at the extreme rear and not threatening anybody or being threatened by anybody—had nonetheless found it necessary to divine a rut and tip over. "Race drivers are the wreckers of race cars!" Dennie's contorted puss seemed to say. The old refrain.

By then the sun had gone down and it was too dark to complete the missing 11 miles, so the 1961 Phoenix ended. Everyone seemed relieved except Don Branson, who, fit as a fiddle on the minefield track, and coming on like a locomotive, might well have caught Parnelli and won, had the 100 miles gone to conclusion.

Rodger's Repeat and the Saga of Knothead

Reporters are supposed to report, not wear blinders. Looking back, commandment 11 was an awful way to learn how to write, and we dirt track hacks were much like the NASCAR shills of Y2K covering the Winston Cup. On the other hand, I'm not sure that dirt track racing could have survived the scrutiny of a full-disclosure press because behavior and disasters that were routinely accepted by racing would never have flown in the real world. Speaking in my self-defense, race drivers, too, were in denial and saw only the speak-no-ill-of-racing side. When, for instance, Jimmy Bryant bought it at Langhorne, the racer-dictated ethos of 1951–1971 demanded that racing be defended at all costs and that blame not get placed on Langhorne but on Jimmy's alleged over-the-hill wheelmanship. Eddie Sachs said so publicly.

"Marble orchard," the boneyard euphemism, was just one of their user-friendly terms that put a jaunty spin on anything bad. "Oops!" was another. An "oops!" covered everything from a harmless spinout to a disaster like Al Keller's. Rodger Ward, runner-up to Parnelli at Phoenix, and almost the only champion of 1951–1971 who was a hard racer throughout both decades, was entitled to wonder if the Phoenix "oops!" hadn't been a bizarre replay of an almost identical "oops!" of eight years prior.

It happened in 1953 in Detroit, at the Michigan State Fairgrounds, and was the first champ car win of Rodger's career 26, and the one he once said he least

Eddie Sachs was one of the foremost defenders of the speak-no-evil of racing credo. *Bob Tronolone*

The unbelievable Knothead Heath. He played rope-a-dope with every crashwall from Seattle to San Diego, surviving and prospering by observing twin dictums, or Heathisms: 1) "Drive a race car like you ain't got a cent invested in it," and 2) "Where the front end goes, the back end follows!" *Bob Tronolone*

liked to claim. Had Detroit not ultimately gotten banished from the championship calendar, it might well have joined Phoenix and Langhorne as the tourney's third mile-track from hell. Detroit was damn near impossible. The unyielding surface pounded Kurtis-Krafts and Kuzmas to bits, and you couldn't see for the dust. Flying equipment sometimes made unscheduled appearances in spectator zones, too, as when an endoing midget cleared a fence and annihilated the prize equine of Detroit's police drill squadron.

Detroit, 1953, presented the foulest conditions ever. First the track surface blew up in everyone's faces, and

next the automobiles began jumping, dancing, and bounding so high that drivers were rendered acrophobic.

At 51 miles the sanctioning American Automobile Association interrupted the proceedings with the red flag. Rodger and the madman known as "Knothead"— Allen Heath—were running first and second and assumed, thankfully, that racing was concluded. But after dumping on a little water, the standard collection of choleric coot stewards who were running things ordered Rodger, Knothead, and the seven other surviving shell-shocked combatants back to their pulverized sleds. The show must go on!

Arguing that the racetrack was a piece of crap that was going to destroy them all, the drivers (unlike their colleagues at Phoenix eight years later, who seemed bigger risk takers) refused. The drivers were risking draconian punishment, because they were expected to race on the tracks they were given, and their iron authority gave the coots the privilege to put down the slightest driver insubordination by revoking competition licenses. But the drivers stood firm anyway, and the coots, for once, capitulated. Racing would resume, but the standings at 51 miles would be official, and all everyone need do for 49 laps was parade slowly and look nice for the Detroit crowd.

Yet even parade lap speeds were sufficient for one of the craters to rip a wheel off Rodger's falling-to-pieces *M.A. Walker Special* and impale it on a fence, giving the race lead to Knothead; a bit later Detroit sent a second sacrificial car on its top and its driver to the fracture ward. Racing then got red-flagged a second time and for good. In the aftermath, instead of explaining why Rodger—his *M.A. Walker* still hanging on the wall—had won, and Knothead, in the lead, had lost, everything was stealthily bottomed up into another "oops!"

Knothead Heath was a fascinating case. One of dirt's unsung stalwarts, he was a naughty actor midget maestro

Parnelli, leading, and Mel Kenyon match 1964 doodlebug moves. Mel later sacrificed an arm to an Indy car blaze, but emulated Knothead Heath and enjoyed a long and dazzlingly successful second career competing with an artificial limb. *Bob Tronolone*

137

Herk's decision to mount a spare tank of volatile methanol right in the nose of his Indy roadster, coupled with USAC's willingness to allow him to, was yet another example of an "oops." Herk forever bore the scars of it. But never whined about it. *Bob Tronolone*

Rodger Ward (opposite). His early nickname was "Rodger the Dodger" for his good fortune ducking wrecks that were breaking out all around him. *Bob Tronolone*

whose nickname derived from Heath's playing rope-a-dope with the lumber crash barriers of every sod saucer from Seattle to San Diego. He got into doodlebug spills he was lucky to survive, but the big crackpot caper that could well have finished Knothead occurred at a hardtop show. He and the local favorite driver commenced to bammin' and frammin' until Knothead got crowded into the infield; laying for the local favorite afterward, he proceeded to park him on the wall. And then Knothead ground his own hardtop into reverse to back up slam-bam into the local favorite for good measure.

Serious mistake. The partisan crowd, previously docile, lost its head and turned hooligan and came surging onto the track to get at Knothead, who exacerbated a bad situation into a crisis by yelling defiance at his would-be attackers. Punches were thrown and a few landed; cops began escorting Knothead off the track in the safety of a black and white, whereupon Knothead apparently popped off a second time and sent the crowd into so heated a fury they attempted to roll over the cruiser with Knothead in it.

Knothead hit the dirt track highway to Indy the same time as Rodger, Vookie, and Rutt, but at first got lost in that hypertalented gang and twice missed connecting at the Brickyard. Belatedly, he became the life of the party. In L.A., using a jumped-up rail, the *Vince Conze Offy*, he unseated Jimmy Bryan. Over east, he joined the legends by hosing down Hinnershitz at Reading. In the Midwest, in a midget 100 lapper at DuQuoin, he took down Bill Schindler.

But right after the 1953 Detroit, out in the sticks at Illiana Speedway, the talented Knothead made a slip and had his own "oops!" He was tooling a sprinter whose sloppy mechanics had installed the spindles backwards. They fell out, the car crashed, and Knothead's hurts were major league, including compound fractures to both legs and a shattered left wrist. Croakers at the pathetic little hospital may have done a poor job of cleansing, and later, when gangrene set in, knife-happy surgeons amputated Knothead's hand and substituted a chrome hook.

He was forever finished in the big leagues of 3-A, and so back in L.A. he invented a whole new career for himself as a spellbinder with that chrome hook. Knothead's wheelhouse technique was like nobody else's, ever. United Racing Association midgets and ponderous California Racing Association sprinters carried no power-assisted steering, and Knothead weighed but a ghostly 100 pounds and change. Even so, he taught

You could have a mechanical "oops!" too. Al Unser has just done a thorough job of ventilating the Meyer-Drake in his *Retzloff Chemical* Dunlop.
Bob Tronolone

himself how to place his sound right hand on the steering wheel, just above his belly button, and do all his grappling one-handed. Deploying the hook solely for windmilling and showboating, he ducked, dodged, darted, and as ever, kissed crashwalls while streaking one-armed to countless main event victories of 15-miles, and once even had the impossible stamina to snag a 500.

It was a 1958 novelty marathon road race for V-8-60 Ford midget buzz jobs around the long road course at Riverside International Raceway and Knothead was going like a bomb. So was Herk Hurtubise, a baby hot shoe barely two years away from standing racing on its nose with his almost-sub-minute journey around Indy.

Locking into Knothead man-to-man for nearly all 500 miles, Herk ultimately blew his cool atop the RIR esses and got plugged backward into the railing. Knothead's subsequent victory yelp following the grueling six hours with Herkie was one for posterity: "Hell of a warm-up! Now when do we go racin'?"

Tyrant Time

Racing itself couldn't be blamed for every "oops!" Those tyrant codger potentates of 3-A and later USAC set off quite a few themselves.

Racing's historic weakness for gerontocracy and tyrannical leaders was born in the 1930s with the reign of Arthur Pillsbury, formerly a timber track tycoon.

Not only was Knothead Heath physically tiny, but he looked old, almost wizened. This apparent feebleness was deceptive. Throughout the 1960s, on full-moon sprint car Saturday nights at Ascot Park, you'd see Knothead down in the pits with a paper cup of steaming coffee in his good hand, a cigarette burning in his hook, and a wild look in his eyes. Caffeine, nicotine, and hell-raising motivated him, and whenever Knothead got loose with the Famighetti or Bromme Offys, or the big Miletich 409-inch T-Bird, he was obviously having tremendous fun getting into outrageous sideways postures, then snapping everything back straight again. When he was really going, he spared nobody, especially the race starters and corner marshals he intimidated by chasing to the safety of the infield. Upon winning eight consecutive California Racing Association main events, he celebrated by riding the heavy Famighetti to the top of Ascot's infield motorcycle ramp, then flying off the end: the crash landing snapped the driveshaft, all four springs, and corkscrewed Knothead's spine sufficiently to earn him a stay in an infirmary. Pinching nurses in the tush with his hook almost led to his prompt ejection. *George Johnstone, Scalzo collection*

Ruling by terror was Art's special deal and he and his lieutenants operated less as racing's handmaidens and more like racing's Praetorian guard. "Conduct detrimental to racing" was Art's rubric, covering everything from showing up with a dirty race car to speaking unflatteringly of the 3-A, and either offense could get you hauled in front of a Pillsbury star chamber and lashed with a suspension from all racing competition for up to two years. Holding the unholy distinction of being the 3-A dictator official who presided over the 1934 massacre at Imperial was but one of Art's accomplishments: he additionally trained as a pupil despot the stuffed-shirt Beverly Hills banker who later got Troy Ruttman suspended right in Rutt's prime—an "oops!" if ever there was one.

Having a pack of angry old bully stewards falling on him was rotten luck for any driver, but for Wally Campbell it was worse than that. It turned him into an "oops!"

Wally and Herk Hurtubise never met that I know of—Wally was several years older—but the two led racing existences almost identically urgent and madcap, and they also shared those same sparkler eyes. Growing up in Patterson, New Jersey, Wally earned nickels by lying prone so that elements of the Joie Chitwood Thrill Show could vault over him on their Harley hogs. Shipped to the South Pacific on a warship for World War II, Wally survived the trauma of a fierce firefight that completely blew up the warship. Home in Jersey again and looking for a racing career, he found categories like midgets and sprinters struggling to regain their prewar strengths, so he bored into the new game: taxicab racing. He also fell under Langhorne's spell and developed his dirt witchcraft bouncing modified-stocks around the 'Horne: in three seasons he won 137 American Stock Car Racing Association features and three national titles.

He had a black and movin' Olds 88 that he qualified fastest at NASCAR's first Southern 500 at Darlington, but the dirt track highway was Wally's catnip, and Indy and its 500 were where he most wanted to be. In 1953, abandoning door-slammers, he treated himself to an open-wheel apprenticeship of sorts in NASCAR's short-lived Speedway division by racing his own Nash and later flathead Mercury-powered Hillegass. Next he swamped 3-A's East Coast sprints. He got the chair in the *Frank Curtis Offy*, one of the fastest

One of the saddest "oopses!" was that of Dick Atkins. Just three weeks after he got his rookie career up and flying with a victory in the Sacramento 100, he became the second victim of the mysterious Don Branson incident at Ascot Park on November 12, 1966. *Bob Tronolone*

stretched midgets, and then became Johnny Thomson's teammate on the mighty Sam Traylor squad.

Lightning flashed—or perhaps it was Wally's eyes? In barely 12 months Wally was in the process of completely changing how sprinters were supposed to be raced on dirt. He attacked a steering wheel so spectacularly that his exertions sometimes ripped his shirt in two. The effort was worth it; he tossed off long and dazzling broadslides that not even Jud Larson might have matched. Also in the Campbell repertoire was the

ability—and unworldly reflexes—to cock the steering wheel to full lock, let go, recalibrate arms, then quick-like-hell grab another handful of lock.

Thomson, Hinnershitz, Mike Nazaruk, and other constellations from the formidable East Coast galaxy were having their minds blown by Wally. Unfortunately for Wally, and for us, Wally had to discover—as Herk subsequently did—that eyes like his don't make life easier.

At the 1954 Indy he got permission to take a rookie test, flunking out hugely. It wasn't surprising. Wally was

Langhorne has always had a disproportionate number of "oopses." Pat O'Connor and Jerry Hoyt throttle past the chaos of the 1955 get-together of Sam Traylor teammates Johnny Thomson (standing beside his car) and Al Keller (on his nob). *Bruce Craig*

in a shitbox, for one thing, and another thing was that two of the driver-judges who 86'd him were veteran hacks still not over having Wally kick their butts every day the previous summer at a big St. Paul sprinter match. And as a last nail in Wally's coffin, an inflamed brigade of autocratic 3-A dunces from the Midwest declared that Wally and his way-out East Coast reputation made them uneasy. Wally was instructed to climb down off the dirt highway and go learn how to be a race driver on the local friendly hills of Salem, Winchester, and Dayton.

Wally took the bad advice to heart. The suspended and disgraced Ruttman was then living in eccentric exile near Salem, so Wally sought out Rutt. Making common cause with a fellow outcast, Rutt befriended Wally and upon watching Wally rim Salem decided that he was perhaps the most gifted young race driver he'd ever seen. But Wally had a dirt track soul, not a

slant track soul, and in his inexperience got carried away, or maybe something on his car snapped. He lurched backward out of Salem, and it was all over (Herk went backward out of Dayton once, wasn't injured, and never came back). Ruttman went home, called a wake for Wally, and everyone got drunk marking still another "oops!"—for my money, the most unforgivable one of the lot.

Wally's family later had the 3-A's Contest Board weasel out of paying death benefits on the pretext that because Wally's demise hadn't occurred in a race, there was no obligation to pay. It was insult to injury, but the widows and survivors of dirt track drivers were a wretched subgenre anyway. In fact, why not come out and admit it? They were the ones always taking it in the neck. They never received much comfort from an "oops!"

Tyrant 3-A officials were permitted to remain in harness for so long that some outlasted the oldest

Minnesota State Fair, 1959, and yet another bad moment, this one costing the life of Little Jim Gilchrist, No. 77. Jim Hurtubise flashes past, typically untouched. *Al Herman, Jake Bozony collection*

race cars. Were the old SOBs eternal? It was a hideous thought.

Then in the ultra-bad-ink summer of 1955, when Vookie's Brickyard departure was the highest profile of perhaps half a dozen "oops!" the 3-A, after five decades of misery, fled racing. The U.S. Auto Club, USAC, became the new democratic fraternity serving the sport.

Pappy Carter, USAC's first director of competition, formerly a top shoe on dirt and paving alike, ran the show like he was in a race. He set his sights on Italy and got the champ cars invited to Monza. He made a tire supplier commit to building the proper rubber so that Indy might host a 500-mile taxicab bonanza. He traveled to Bonneville to see how USAC could take over the salt nationals, and he ventured to the high altitudes of Pikes Peak to create a USAC hill-climbing division. Rim-riding and pounding the pedal like a good dirt tracker, Pappy seemed to be winning his race to make USAC Maximum Leader of All Known Racing until he was fired in 1959. USAC's nervous board of directors decided Pappy wasn't grasping democratic equalitarian concepts.

Neither would the next director of competition, Henry Banks, although initial hopes were high. A former national champion, Henry was known to be soft-spoken, even softhearted. Perhaps the most telling anecdote about kind Henry was this: in 1951, during an especially crash-ravaged meet at Syracuse, where Andy Linden was lying injured on the track too numb or scared to move and everyone else continued racing anyway—the 3-A stewards forgot to throw a caution yellow—it had been softie Henry who'd stopped his own crate to suggest that something ought to be done about poor Andy. And so something eventually was. The 3-A dispatched a meat wagon going in the wrong direction and four more drivers, including Bill Schindler and Jack McGrath, cracked up trying to miss it.

Sadly, once Henry was installed in office, a fearful metamorphosis occurred. USAC's sash of authority quickly turned the soft-hearted former driver into a railing and capricious zealot who made life under Art Pillsbury and the AAA seem like the good old days.

Corporal punishment bloomed: Henry and his USAC lieutenants hung a big financial fine on Jim Hurtubise after catching Herk using potty-mouth language. Eddie Sachs, at a Phoenix race, tried and failed to get an extra pit pass for the wife of his chief mechanic, Wally Meskowski, mouthed off in protest, and was refused permission to race at all. Typically, A. J. Foyt survived the heat best. Exactly why USAC chose to clamp down on its hottest product was a mystery, but after A. J. was alleged to have thrown a headlock on Johnny White and then flipped off the spectators at a Williams Grove sprint meet, USAC treated A. J., too, to a turn in the stocks. A. J. got suspended from racing on a Tuesday, unsuspended on a Thursday, and then resuspended on a Monday. Henry Banks called the full 19-member USAC board into session for a special punishment hearing where A. J., who came out shooting, denied everything. Demanding that he be given a lie detector exam, he made Henry and the board capitulate. Encore! What a show!

Yet the Looney Tunes show of Elmer George vs. USAC during and after the 1959 Langhorne had come close to exceeding it.

Elmer Ray George—nobody now seems to remember who the "Ray" in the family tree was—arguably had the most humble beginnings of any future famous 1951–1971 player. His forebears were refugees of dust bowl Oklahoma who relocated to central California and led a ritzy existence in one of the Depression's most miserable squatters' camps. This camp, called Alisol, outside of Salinas in the coastal San Joaquin Valley, was where Elmer got into the itinerant lettuce business—he picked it. Moving up in the chain of command, he later trucked it to market.

But then Elmer found racing and took off on the migrant dirt track highway to Indy. Like Eddie Sachs and others before him, Elmer began campaigning the prime equipment of the Mari Hulman stable—legend has it that Mari came into $14 million when she turned 21 and that she promptly purchased her first sprinter—but unlike the other drivers, Elmer subsequently courted, won, and wed the stable's owner.

You can afford lots of race cars with a budget of $14 million (and a lot more where that came from), so if anyone appeared to have it made, it was Elmer. It would have been nice if he'd possessed the same talents as racing's other speedy Okie, Troy Ruttman, but Elmer did not. His driving was a bit baffling.

Although Elmer had no trepidation whatsoever about going into the belly of the beast on the slant tracks—one season he became their seasonal champion—he could not race well on miles or at his father-in-law's Indianapolis. He was inaccurate. At DuQuoin the day he defeated Parnelli Jones for the first and only time, Elmer goofed up and committed the scandal of bumping into and overturning Don Branson—Don got so angry about it that during the rollovers he prayed he'd live just so he could go ice Elmer afterward. Aggression always counted more than patience. Elmer got so overwrought at his maiden Indy 500 that he disabled two Offy roadsters, one of them his own. This might have been forgivable, except that it occurred while everyone was just trying to get lined up for the pace lap.

Elmer was gullible, too, and trickster Rodger Ward really hung him out to dry at the 1957 Springfield 100. Fireball George Amick was on pole, Elmer was lined up next to him on the outside, and Rodger was behind Elmer on row two. "If that Amick gets loose, we'll never see him," Rodger told Elmer, drawing Elmer into a conspiracy where Elmer was supposed to keep Amick pinned at the start. Rodger stratagems invariably worked and, sure enough, as the field plunged for turn one, Elmer bit on Rodger's bait and plugged up Amick by swerving low. And this broke the top groove wide open with blue skies just when Rodger needed it. Rodger won in a runaway and Elmer was left among the backmarkers.

Elmer had a temper, but sometimes that helped him. During a tense sprint-car Sunday afternoon at Reading,

Elmer qualified a poor 11th fastest, angrily dropped out of the opening scratch heat, took a mediocre fifth in the second, spun out of the third, and had to desperately overcome half a dozen cars in the consie just to transfer to the feature. Then he gave himself a stiff talking to and smashed icon Jud Larson to win it.

Langhorne, 1959, was the brawl of Elmer's life. And it was a really great 'Horne 100, without gore for a change. Jud, Sachs, Branson, and all the other major players were on form, but Elmer was on a flier. He was leading at 23 miles, had lapped up to sixth place by 40. But by then the nervous Nellie USAC stewards were worried that Elmer's ragged driving was looking even more ragged than normal. Scared shitless that he was about to do himself a serious injury, they wrung their hands, cogitated, and at last hung the black disqualification flag on Elmer!

It was Langhorne's 73rd mile. Elmer by then had lapped everyone but second place. Maybe never before had any leader been hauled off a dirt track merely for looking out of control, but Elmer's rotten luck was that he wasn't just "any" leader: he was Tony Hulman's son-in-law, and should the bastard yellow press get hold of a juicy story about Elmer getting snuffed, well, the thunderstorm of negative headlines and black ink could drown all racing! Tony might even close the Speedway! So apparently went USAC's tortured thinking process.

For 11 laps Elmer caused a huge stink by choosing to ignore, or not see, the black flag. Temper time clicked in when he finally did decide to stop, and Elmer ended up clipping the steward who was refusing to return his competition license. Interestingly, this particular steward wasn't the standard USAC coot but a whippersnapper Elmer's own age and of Elmer's mentality. So the two of them cordially agreed to meet down in Langhorne's dank catacombs tunnel to adjudicate matters by going to fist city a second time.

They didn't go through with it, and what a pity things weren't settled that way. Instead, gerontocracy

Mari Hulman's *HOW Special* of 1955 was the former *Bessie Lee Paoli Springfield Welding* Kurtis-Kraft. Left to right, mechanic/builder Bob DeBisschop, Elmer George, Mari Hulman, and mother, Mary. *Scalzo collection*

kicked in again. Back at the USAC headquarters in Indianapolis, the old guys decided that Elmer was a rockhead in need of serious discipline and that he must stand before a geezer star chamber, with one of his inquisitors none other than the original hanging judge of racing magistrates, Art Pillsbury. This coot tribunal subsequently threw the book at Elmer, fining him a pretty buck and suspending him until he paid up. Elmer retorted that he'd never pay, and with Mari and the race cars departed to lead an exile's life barnstorming with the IMCA.

In time somebody paid Elmer's fine and Elmer returned to USAC. But he kept getting into more hot water, including back at Langhorne, where he and another relief driver struggled to subdue the hoodooed *Vargo Special*, and only Elmer emerged alive; and at Phoenix where Elmer veered right on the front straight and got into the spectator bleachers. After this, spouse Mari divested herself of her stable, and Elmer got out of the cockpit to became part of the Indianapolis management, though not too big a part. First he was put to work as a kind of assistant groundskeeper, then promoted to a vice presidency—but

only of the Speedway Radio Network. Following the completion of the 500's 60th edition, Elmer was assigned to take the pace car and escort the winner, our buddy Johnny Rutherford, around the Speedway.

This time no earthly black flag flew for Elmer, but Fate had decided that Elmer's days were through—racing and otherwise. Less than a dozen hours after chauffeuring Johnny casually around the Brickyard, Elmer George was dead.

The details of Elmer's downfall on May 30, 1976, remain murky. Mari had filed for divorce and Elmer's life was turning to junk. Typically angry and this time carrying a firearm, he had rushed to Terre Haute to take extreme measures dislodging a defiant tenant from a Hulman estate there. Elmer succeeded in getting off two rounds but the tenant, a quarter-horse trainer stationed on the second story, fired five. A Vigo County grand jury took only a week to rule justified homicide.

Elmer obits in all the Indianapolis dailies were brief. And that was a loss; dirt track actors don't come any hotter.

Elmer George and his Kurtis/Watson, the HOW, which began life as the *Springfield Welding*, 1952 national champion 3-A car. It also won the 1953 Sacramento 100—Jimmy Bryan's breakthrough win on a mile—and in 1957 Elmer really stood up in the seat and set a new track record nailing Syracuse. *Bob Tronolone*

Another typical right-of-way dispute at Imperial. *George Johnstone, Scalzo collection*

Looking back, my favorite example of this apparently honorable-yet-flawed tradition of turning old dirt track drivers into mad-dog officials is Babe Stapp. Babe was a long-time friend as well as the father of Steve Stapp, one of the truly "alive" sprint car team owners of the 1960s. Once a ranking chauffeur in his own distant day, which was the 1920s and 1930s, Babe's big officiating caper went down in 1958, at a high-llama professional Grand Prix at the same Riverside Raceway where Knothead Heath once made his great midget run. USAC in 1958 was trying to muscle in on the dilettantes of la-di-dah sporty car racing and Babe was a steward in the pits.

Among the star entrants was a team of V-8 Scarabs belonging to exotic blueblood Lance Reventlow, whose father was a prince and whose mother was a Woolworth department store millionairess. So far, so good. But Babe, upon noting Lance's personal Scarab leaking gasoline, exercised his USAC steward's privilege to punish and disqualified Lance from further racing. Lance and his clique of ego-trippers couldn't understand the tradition of genuflecting to ex-dirt tracker authority. Protesting, Lance spiked his helmet at Babe's feet. And next he told him off with language that Babe was startled a blueblood would know. Attempting to regain order the only way he knew, Babe pitched a thundering haymaker at Lance.

I was present at this Grand Prix, and regretted that Babe's haymaker missed—I thought Lance had it coming. Anyway, Babe was already a racing folk hero venerated for the role he played in rescuing Lil Triplett in that original Imperial/Forest Lawn business so well remembered and feared by Jim Lunt.

That fine moment for Babe occurred back on March 6, 1934, which had dawned miserably sad in L.A. In the afternoon Babe had been one of the many racing men wearing black filing into the mausoleum at Forest Lawn to say goodbye to Ernie Triplett, the most celebrated of three victims wiped out the previous weekend at Imperial.

Conducted under Art Pillsbury's watch, Imperial's feature race was run on a dust-blind track, without 3-A stewards flagging the corners, and with a derelict car left parked on the track. The inevitable crash included Triplett among its casualties and flushed out an inexperienced first-aid crew that didn't even have an ambulance. Improvising, they tossed the injured and dying into the bed of a farmer's pickup truck and set out across the vast hinterlands of the Coachella Valley in search of the nearest hospital.

At Forest Lawn, swirling around Babe and the other mourners, was a wolf pack of attack hacks, sob sisters, and hit-and-run photogs from *The Herald Examiner*, L.A.'s William Randolph Hearst paper. And Ernie's widow, a portrait of bereavement, was buzzed on all sides. The hacks bumped her, the sob sisters—chick reporters who literally sobbed with their victims—engulfed her, and busybody lensmen surrounded her.

From the other side of the mausoleum, Babe and Ernie's other hardliner colleagues observed the behavior of the Hearstians. Babe, his face well seasoned from the blows of crashwall planks, was the worst hardliner of the bunch, despite his back being imprisoned in a brace after he'd gotten careless in a Wednesday sprint match at Legion Ascot Speedway. Not surprisingly, the spectacle of Lil Triplett being harassed caused Babe's sentimental heart to open in sympathy. He rounded up additional hardliners and issued the order to charge.

Ejected from Forest Lawn with oaths, punches, and kicks were a pair of photogs who next got hurled into a waiting car and sped over the Hollywood Hills to receive additional oaths, blows, and kicks before getting dumped on the front steps of the *Examiner*. Now the fat was in the fire. Babe and the others had walked blindly into Hearst's grasp.

Racers Kidnap 2 Newsmen, Face Charges

". . . Gangster tactics that desecrated the sacred soil of the cemetery . . . courageous driver whose life was sacrificed . . . vicious beating of a photographer (a World War veteran) . . ."

There was no tradition of responsibility in popular journalism, so William Randolph displayed no restraint. He began jumping up and down on all racing, but his primo target became Legion Ascot, the mystique-covered bowl of macadam that stood on the heights behind L.A. that was kind of the left coast Langhorne of the 1930s.

The despised William Randolph owned 29 other papers besides the *Examiner*, plus 15 magazines; he was the most powerful publisher in the world. And he had sympathetic friends. A city superintendent tried stopping L.A. County Hospital from accepting Legion Ascot participants on the grounds that they were only suicide chasers anyway. A legislator hinted darkly at plans to reintroduce Bill No. 5, infamously known as the "ban racing" measure. And a hostile district attorney suggested Legion Ascot shows be cancelled until all the "kidnappers" turned themselves in. Babe and the others promptly did so, and escaped uncharged. Back brace notwithstanding, Babe still succeeding in behaving noisily and badly, particularly while ruminating about yellow journalism and William Randolph Hearst in particular. Some of what he said could actually be printed.

The hostilities went on for years—long enough for Jim Lunt to never get over them. For a time it appeared racing might win by default. The Hearst yellow press was rapidly becoming known as the Hearst crank press, and William Randolph was slipping into his dotage, going bankrupt, and gradually being removed from control.

But Legion Ascot's finest continued decimating themselves at such a brisk rate that the Speedway simply couldn't escape. Early in 1936, Legion closed down. Then an arsonist torched the grandstands. The *Examiner*'s jeering lead sentence became a journalism classic: "Legion Ascot burned down yesterday at a great saving of human life."

As we will see in the next chapter, it surely was Jim Lunt's worst moment when he was forced to shove commandment 11 and share the same sentiments about the most evocative 1951–1971 name going: Langhorne.

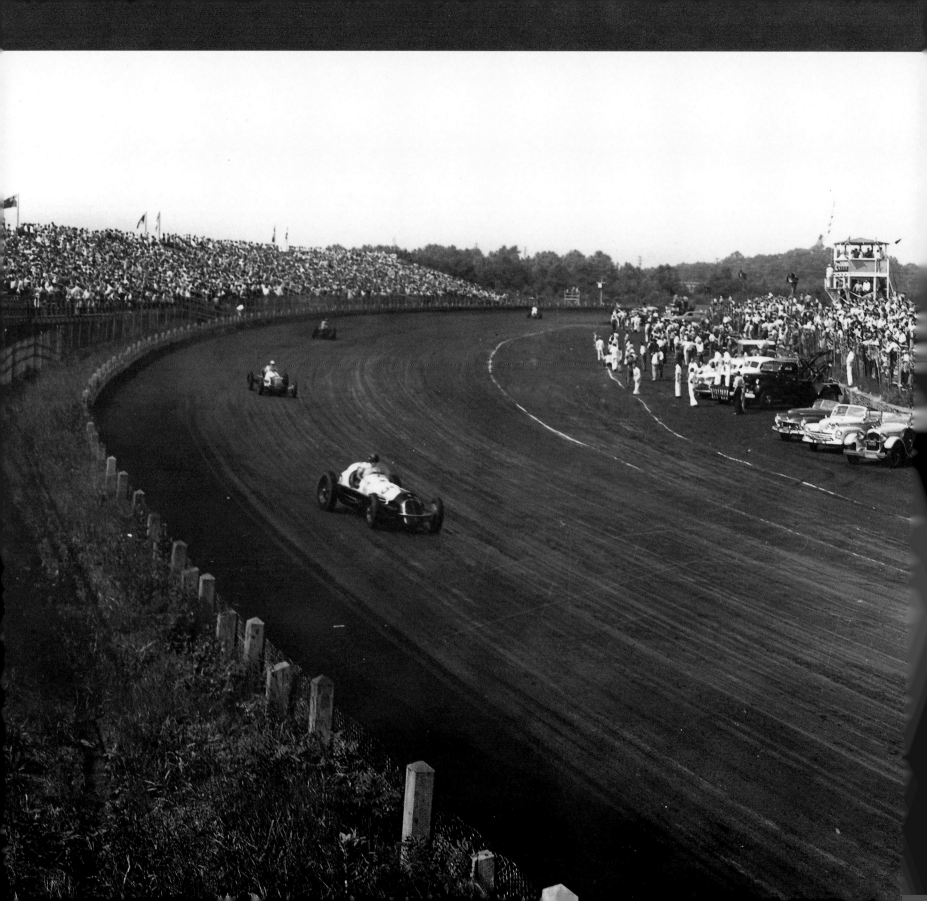

Chapter 5

AT THE 'HORNE

Although it wasn't until the winter of 1964 that Langhorne Speedway, the ultimate dirt track, was pulled down, the 'Horne's last rites were actually written several months earlier, back in the 1964 spring. Jim Lunt penned them.

Paragon Jim was devoted to all dirt racing, but he lived out on the eastern flank of Pennsylvania when it was dirt's hottest precinct, and his passions were Langhorne, Tommy Hinnershitz, and Langhorne. Jim being dirt racing's authority and even conscience, it followed that if Jim was confessing that his own favorite race track needed to be lobotomized with a coat of paving, well, that would just have to be Langhorne's fate. So, reluctantly but firmly bidding "the big left turn" farewell, Jim wrote, "We have felt for a long time that despite the thrilling racing at Langhorne's famous oval—fastest in the world—the danger to drivers of championship cars, sprints, and midgets was too great" (how owning up to that must have twisted Jim's speak-no-evil soul!). "No need to recount here the many fatalities and lucky escapes in crashes recorded at Langhorne in past years. Nor are we criticizing the management of the speedway for track conditions. They tried their utmost to keep the track in good condition but found the second turn to be impossibly rough . . ."

Finally, having always previously written with reverence that race drivers were completely fearless creatures, Jim had to go all the way and confess: "We could (but don't intend to) name several pilots who, despite the fact that they drove there, drove Langhorne with fear in their hearts . . ."

Perhaps only Mike Nazaruk, Charlie Musselman, Jimmy Bryan, Don Branson, A. J. Foyt, and Johnny Thomson—six guys who really ran the track—ever didn't. Flying around the Horne's dark and rutted circle at hurtling speeds while totally exposed in the cockpit and vulnerable from hips to helmet top simply wasn't to everyone's taste, not even the giants.

Tony Bettenhausen conquered the 'Horne during his blitzkrieg 1951, but didn't often return. Rodger Ward usually managed to be several states away whenever Langhorne had something cooking. Jud Larson never quite overcame the place either: it flipped him in 1957, demoralized him enough to make him announce his retirement (later recanted) in 1958, then banged his keister so severely when he did come back in 1964 that afterward he sat exhausted and suckin' wind in his overheated box for almost an hour before at last staggering out of the cockpit.

Hard on it down into Puke Hollow in the Langhorne old days. The 'Horne was Hades on wheels then, too. *Bruce Craig*

Johnny Rutherford once told how the fun 'n' games began long before Langhorne's wicked G-forces kicked in trying to overturn all the race cars. Merely pulling out of the pits and onto the track could turn into a thrill because the 'Horne's beargrease surface was slick enough to slip a car into the wall while it was in bottom gear.

Leroy Neumeyer, pre-Langhorne, had warmed up his cardiac muscles by getting a primitive salt shaker hot rod going almost 300 miles per hour across Bonneville. Later, he strapped on Diz Wilson's *No. 70* and made searing top-lane journeys around such IMCA high-banks as Memphis, Tennessee, where there were no guardrails to keep you inside and a moat to land in if you vaulted outside. Cheap thrills, both. According to Leroy, by far the most fascinating and horrifying piece of racing real estate going—the supremo of heart revver-uppers—was "Puke Hollow," located just after Langhorne's downhill start/finish.

Experiencing firsthand the big rolling swells coming up from its rock bottom, Leroy went pitching ferociously into Puke aboard the *Federal Engineering*, a bounding and antique Kurtis-Kraft, whose deteriorating

front shock absorbers were preparing to follow the example of the rears by blowing out completely.

Anybody coming off Langhorne after going 100 miles in a champ car had glazed-over eyes that seemed to say, "I have seen things nobody else has." Don Branson, who in 1962 established the everlasting record average of nearly 105 miles per hour, could scarcely see at all; he had to spend the night in the infirmary having his ruined eyes swabbed clean. Indeed, so ravaged and worn-out did poor old Don seem—this time not even the usual cargo of vitamins had helped—that he no longer resembled a race driver but a shell-shocked trench soldier from World War I. Was winning any race worth what he'd gone through?

What with a Langhorne driver forced to cock his steering wheel hard-left in a death grip broadside lasting 100 miles, the 'Horne succeeded in reducing the palms of hands to raw and bleeding hamburger. A ravenous appetite for necks du jour was another part of the menu.

Anybody constructing the ideal Langhorne chauffeur wanted a size-13 throttle foot complemented by a draft horse–size neck, but only powerhouses Jimmy

March 20, 1955: Mike Nazaruk, dinged up and in semishock (and dressed in Eddie Sachs' uniform), wears the traditional Langhorne "I have seen things nobody else has," expression. Mike's just won the 3-A sprint car feature that took out Crash Crockett.
Bruce Craig

At times the 'Horne seemed alive with evil spirits rising up and surrounding it. Al Keller survived this 1955 Langhorne wipeout at the cost of a thumb. Langhorne exploited weakness and demanded an unfair amount of pain.
Walt Imlay, Stew Reamer collection

Bryan and A. J. Foyt met those specs. Langhorne ate up and spit out tiny George Amick in only 30 miles in 1955—although George and another of those wonder Kuzmas came back to win in 1956. And for somebody like slender Bobby Marshman—who had only a long, thin neck to support his helmeted head and hold it upright in the face of all the centrifugal forces—100 miles of Langhorne was equally frazzling. In fact, just 50 miles of Langhorne was.

The first segment of a 1963 "Twin 50s" sprint car session left Bobby and his frail neck so physically debilitated that car owner Don Shepherd suffered a typical panic attack of conscience and refused to put Bobby

Herkie just drove right past all of 'em in a 1960 Langhorne 50-mile sprinter (above). Afterward, weighed down with accumulated Langhorne grime, he looked like it had been a 500-miler (left). *Bruce Craig*

back into the car for the second 50 unless Bobby's wife OK'd it. She did; whereupon Bobby—to Shep's applauding approval—somehow summoned the inner wherewithal to hold the hammer down and keep his weak neck upright for all 50 miles.

Race car rigors were comparable to driver rigors. An especially eloquent testament to 'Horne destruction was the Plymouth MoPar, a big hemi, used by Herk Hurtubise to win a 150-mile taxicab feature. Herk hit victory circle with a shattered windshield, rubber smears and scars on both flanks, and a section of wooden Langhorne guardrail stuck into a rear quarter-panel. And that, mind you, was a battleship 'cab, not one of those flexing, flyweight, stretched-midget sprinters like Mike

Nazaruk's *Nyquist Offy* that were so gristly that in pinwheeling wrecks they reduced themselves to rubble, throwing axles and even sometimes their drivers.

Langhorne also made the big champ cars moan as if they were in real pain. Tires were the first component to go and even when a chief mechanic underinflated to 35 pounds, the right rear Firestone block tread or diamond was bound to cook; even 55 pounds often wouldn't save one. Shock absorber, torsion bar, and radius rod failures followed, and throughout the 100 miles all of the buzzing, complaining Meyer-Drakes wondered what the hell kind of race track Langhorne was that it forced them to pull so hard up the back-straight and then plunge too easily into Puke

Purveyors of chills-down-the-spine racing, a quartet of Langhorne grapplers try to avoid creaming each other. They are: Jiggs Peters, Roger McCluskey, Elmer George, and Rex Easton. *Bruce Craig*

Hollow. Puke, incidentally, wasn't so named because scared drivers tossed their cookies there. It was because all the extra speed made engines regurgitate rods, pistons, and whatnot.

If a Langhorne driver was lucky, he finished, if he was unlucky his car broke, and if he was extra unlucky he messed up and crashed. Most Langhorne crashes were choice, if that is the word. The 1951 chain-reaction, multimachine masher that Wally Campbell got in the middle of during his modified-taxicab days was so huge that on film it looks like racing's first nonending wreck. Yet no matter how much a sled was hurting, its driver was expected to bring it home. And if the driver

wore himself out trying, he was supposed to stop and be replaced by somebody else. Often a driver might stop for relief and have no fresh driver willing to show up to supply it. Conversely, driving relief at Langhorne started some careers. And ended others.

But the important rough-justice etiquette was that cars continue circling Langhorne no matter what. Roger McCluskey, dirt track racing's most black-humored—and funniest—man, once told in hilarious McCluskeyesque detail the story of his engrossing 1962 Langhorne ride in the same hastily rebuilt *Bell Lines Trucking* that A. J. Shepherd had savagely wrecked at the Hoosier Hundred.

June 2, 1957, at Langhorne was Johnny Thomson's biggest day. Perhaps it was dirt racing's biggest one too. Bad Man scored the breath-catching win many drivers might have traded a whole career for. *Bob Tronolone*

Wondering what had happened to Buster Warke, his chief mechanic, and why Buster had stopped blackboarding him pit signals, Roger saw that it was because Buster was in the middle of an intense powwow with one of the USAC stewards. The conversation had something to do with the *Bell*, because every time Roger careened past, Buster and the steward were staring and gesturing toward its front end. Then they dropped down into crouches to stare and gesture all the harder. Then the steward took out a pair of binoculars, and he and Buster shared them, continuing to stare and gesturing at the front end. Nothing turned out to be wrong with *Bell*, but the pantomime went on for the rest of the race: Buster and the steward continuing to stare and gesture, Roger's head filling with lurid fantasies of the entire front end flying free while he bulled into Puke Hollow.

Additionally, there was the sweltering Langhorne sun. Every 'Horne 100 was conducted around June or July, so the weather was hot, Phoenix-hot. Reflecting up off the Speedway's glaring black surface, the 100-degree temps zapped cars and drivers equally and without predjudice. Spectators up in the uncovered main seating section across from start/finish took a frying as well, especially poor old Jim Lunt, whose health was somewhat shaky anyway.

"The sun seems to wait for race day at the 'Horne—at which times he burns more fiercely every minute," Jim wrote. And: "The crowd and purse set a record, and it's my bet the heat did too, old sol being a race fan for certain. He parked right over the track until the checkered fell, then headed west."

A Jim Lunt column occasionally requested politely that Langhorne's tightwad management consider roofing their dilapidated open grandstands. Request denied! Suffering was universal, it seemed part of the Langhorne mystique: paying patrons had to take it like everybody else.

Temps were so torturing that they might have left the Horne's black dirt burning—which it already was for drivers, especially those who ever had to do the eye-rinse number. Only Atlanta's blood-red gumbo was so hard on cars, and the accumulated black guck resisted mere detergent-scrubbing or steam-cleaning. Chief mechanics and their gofers sometimes chipped away at it for days, finally having to repaint anyway. The 'Horne's mean surface was easily explained. As a cut-rate means of taming dust storms, management routinely had contractors pump vast reservoirs of used

158

The *Tassi Vatis Kurtis 4000* takes a ride up high against the 'Horne's rampart of dense woods, where only a brave handful ever dared trespass. Chuck Hulse is the intrepid chauffeur. *Bruce Craig*

motor oil and crankcase sludge onto the track. Essentially, drivers were putting their cars and lives at risk upon a slick witch's brew of toxic waste.

So why was Jim Lunt so pained to see Langhorne go away when it was such a lightning rod for calamity and destruction? Why at Langhorne's finale did fans take home brown bags filled with souvenir scoops of contaminated black earth as last mementos? Why even today do certain 1951–1971-era drivers and mechanics and diehards still pine for the evil old 'Horne?

For the same reason that road racers deplore the passing of such wonders/horrors as the Mexican Road Race, the Mille Miglia, and the original Nurburgring and Spa-Francorchamps. The 'Horne was just about the last of the really difficult, ennobling race tracks, and watching the spectacle of a 'Horne 100-miler was like nothing else. Winning must have been even better—surely it was why Don Branson put himself through what he did

Enjoying Langhorne was indefensible, maybe, yet who wouldn't have? There was no other track anywhere where the pack took the green with everybody already fiercely broadsliding, and from the pits you picked out the familiar liveries of Dean Van Lines, D-A Lubricants,

Peter Schmidt, Bowes Seal Fast, and Sheraton-Thompson. The cars dropped into Puke Hollow and fell momentarily out of sight, then reappeared with that engine horror sound as everybody swept to the top of Langhorne's outermost fringe, up where the track merged against a rampart of dense woods. Then everybody fired around, completing mile one with 99 identically incredible ones still to come.

Iron Mike

"A Real Idiot's Delight," Upside-Down Rounds—who loved the place—once described Langhorne. For the right kind of driver, the one who didn't have fear in his heart, there really was no other track. Perhaps for that kind of driver, racing at Langhorne was the equivalent of those blond beach hunks on their ironing boards seeking the euphoria of jumping on top of the frothy curler that becomes "the endless wave."

The 'Horne offered the zing of the endless broadslide, and maybe if he hadn't succumbed to it, Mike Nazaruk, the death-before-dishonor jarhead who was a Langhorne luminary to all, wouldn't have had his favorite track rise up and do him in.

Mike Nazaruk wanted others to like Langhorne as much as he did. After the IMCA star Slats Slater got roughed up by the 'Horne, Mike was immediately up close and personal, explaining to Slats where he'd gone wrong and what he should do next time. "Next time" didn't occur. Slats never returned. *Bruce Craig*

Mike's end came on May 1, 1955, and it was typical of him and his regard for Langhorne that he would be there racing instead of in Indianapolis for the opening of 500 practice. His demise hit hard because he was an irresistible madman who couldn't possibly be replaced—Mike was about 10 times larger than life—and because he was a highly versatile risk-chaser who, along with Bob Sweikert and Eddie Sachs, enjoyed being tested on the slant bowls of Salem, Winchester, and Dayton.

Nobody else was quite so torn up by Mike's departure as hammer-down Lee Elkins, the baron of McNamara Motor Freight and its squad of Indy roadsters, champ dirters, and sprinters. Out of the whole rogue's gallery of McNamara Motor Freight desperado chauffeurs, Mike had been the one closest to big Lee's own reckless heart. Among the perks Lee granted Mike had been the privilege of taking up in the air some of the McNamara company airplanes. Never mind that Mike lacked a license: the kind of flying he did couldn't be taught, and included—there are witnesses—playing chicken with railroad locomotives.

Lee's mourning for Mike was long-lasting, genuine, and wasn't helped by Lee's knowledge that he and Mike had been feuding, and that Mike had just quit McNamara to go race the dubious *Nyquist Offy*. All spruced up with white leather upholstery, and painted gleaming Oldsmobile turquoise and off-white complete with California Kustom flamed nose, the *Nyquist* was the same dubious sprinter that had gotten Wally Campbell. And now Mike. Especially distressing to Lee had been the pitiful reports saying that Mike had done it to himself.

Per reports coming out of Langhorne, Mike had been ill in bed all the previous night, and he arrived at the 'Horne medicated and running a fever. He'd tried alibiing out of having to race, then chose to go through with it. Putting away Charlie Musselman with a chilling move on the 14th lap, and ripping along at a hairy 107-mile-per-hour pace, Mike had typically been in the Langhorne lead until—theory had it—his infirm health caused him to brush the back-straight wall, once, twice, three times. Then he'd gone endo-ing out of the park and the *Nyquist* had added insult to injury by tossing him.

Ego flying high after winning the 1956 Indy 500, Pat Flaherty, who hadn't run dirt tracks in almost a decade, challenged the 'Horne. Pat headed out of the groove and into the fence, shedding a tire that grazed George Amick. Reaching his pit, Pat had no right front doughnut plus a flattened right rear. *Bruce Craig*

But Charlie Musselman had a much different theory . . .

The popular line on Mike was that nothing in racing could possibly spook him after his 2-1/2 years of jungle combat on Guadalcanal, Bougainville, and Kwajalien in World War II. Somehow, though, he'd missed out on the battle of Iwo Jima, and when Mike saw the postage stamp of shot-up fellow marines hoisting the stars and stripes, he supposedly expressed pique that he'd missed out on the job; his mug would have looked good on that stamp.

So it certainly would have, because Mike was smiling and devil-may-care. He subsequently got to do lots of mugging in the winners circle of midget car racing during the late 1940s, although success came hard at first and he had to work on the side as a flower truck jockey.

Mikes's earliest good luck came not from a win but a wreck. Car owner Mike Caruso, looking for a second driver for his team—the best one in the East—came to Freeport Stadium to check out the talent. Perhaps overanxious because he was being watched, Mike turned over and came down in the grandstands, but Caruso and his son Bif hired him anyway. The team leader was the great Bill Schindler, who could dominate Mike at first, just as Bronco did everybody in the 1940s. But Mike reportedly got the Schindler monkey off his back by lining up last in a 100-lapper and then gassing with such intensity on the way to finishing second that he blew right past Bronco without even knowing it.

At the same time that left coast honchos, led by Vookie and Rutt, were bringing midget licks to the Indy 500, Mike interrupted their party by getting to the Brickyard first in 1951 and as a rookie running a very hot second. That set him up, and from then on he raced midgets, sprints, and dirt champs in a fever. In one five-race burst he crashed a sprinter in St. Paul on a Monday, won with a midget in Cincinnati on a Wednesday, raced another midget in Detroit on a Thursday, won with the same midget at DuQuoin on a Saturday, then ran in the top 10 with a champ car at DuQuoin on a Sunday.

Lee Elkins wasn't the only wild-hair car owner who found Mike to be a stimulating companion. Roly-poly Sam Traylor, dirt's funniest, most troublemaking rich kid, too, liked to wind himself up when in Mike's company.

One time Sam and Mike got to scuffling and wrestling in the lobby of an Oklahoma City motel and Sam took advantage of his own 6-foot, 4-inch, 260-pound frame to overpower Mike and dump him upside-down in a potted plant, causing their eviction from the motel. Later the White Front threw the pair of them out when Mike, annoyed that the bar's loud band was drowning out conversation, fetched a grapefruit from the kitchen and stuffed it into the bell of a blaring sax.

And one 1954 midnight, Sam and Mike and Charlie Musselman had been having their own feast of fools at some kind of awards banquet when Mike and Charlie had words. Charlie, all full of beer courage, drilled Mike with a sucker poke that got the pair of them, as well as Sam, tossed out, as usual.

Although not highly regarded outside the East, carrot-topped Charlie was a Langhorne lion who in some quarters was identified as the party who'd first raised the speed bar by demonstrating that the fast line around the 'Horne was on the top. So on fateful May 1, 1955, Charlie made his familiar flanking maneuver to the outside in an attempt to do the 25 miles in 14 minutes.

Just behind him, Mike was coming at full hammer. Ill with flu or not, he and the *Nyquist* came around Charlie with a long fantastic broadslide that missed Charlie by an inch. Ahead of him Charlie watched Mike setting up the *Nyquist* for what Langhorne called turn three. Mike jabbed it; he wrestled with the *Nyquist*. And then the whole car shook and straightened up and took the first of the three wall taps that finished it and Mike.

Charlie couldn't believe it. "So Mike goes out, stands on the gas, and fishtails the first time. Then he stands on the gas and fishtails the second time. And then he stands on it the third time and hooks the wall. Whattaya gonna say about something like that? Huh? Mike is nuts!"

Charlie's theory was that Mike's demise wasn't brought about by flu, but by Mike getting carried away trying to pay back Charlie for that sucker swat. But isn't it also possible that Mike just got carried away with that Langhorne endless-wave euphoria?

Charlie wasn't always playing with a full deck himself. And he was luckier than Mike. Back at Langhorne two years later, in 1957, he was leading and merrily lapping the field—he had the 'Horne euphoria—when his left front wheel hit a slower car and his own sprinter—one of Sam Traylor's—stood on its nose. All seat straps snapped and Charlie was tossed out. He flew for awhile then hit the black track with head, spine, and heels—everything at once—but somehow wasn't hurt, although he was unconscious. Waking up in the meat wagon, he was in his stocking feet; the high-top clodhoppers he'd been wearing were left behind in the car.

With his colorful anticipation of disaster, acrid wit, and sardonic giggle that was a duplicate of James Dean's, Roger McCluskey was the perfect Langhorne voice. *Bob Tronolone*

More Langhorne old days. The 'Horne's having another duster. *Bruce Craig*

Big Jimbo

Much like it had Mike Nazaruk, Langhorne carried away Jimmy Bryan, the colossus of all dirt, and Langhorne's original grand master.

It happened during 1960's 100, when Jimmy broke first and jammed into the lead like old times, even though he hadn't raced a dirt car in 2-1/2 seasons and had been away from Langhorne for 3. At full flight into Puke, his car—A. J. Watson's *Leader Card 1*—appeared to go into the required wildslide, but then was enveloped in a conspiracy that included Branson, Herk, Upside-Down, and Jim Packard. Amidst piercing Offenhauser war whoops, the white *Leader Card* reared

and began overturning. And when all the flipping ended, Jimmy, the almighty emblem of dirt tracking, was gone.

World racing was already numbed—this was the same wicked weekend that Formula One lost two drivers at Spa—but next came shocks and revelations from Rodger Ward and Clint Brawner. Rodger, the *Leader Card's* original driver, claimed that he had warned Jimmy about the automobile's tricky handling: the *Leader Card* was Watson's first four-bar, a finesse car, and therefore hardly Jimmy's cup of tea. And Clint, the chief mechanic who was arguably Bryan's creator, bitterly weighed in next by recounting a strange conversation

that he and Jimmy had just before the green, when Jimmy had seemed abnormally apprehensive.

Put together, the two accounts seemed to say that, truly, Jimmy had done it to himself. He'd let his guard down. And Langhorne, his favorite place in the world, had taken the opportunity to rise up and waste him. RIP Jimbo. Your instincts made you legend; if only you'd heeded them when they told you this once to stay home.

Rodger knew more dirt track tricks; Tony Bettenhausen had more mystique; Bob Sweikert was more unorthodox; lackadaisical Jud, when the spirit moved him, outbroadslid everyone; and the taciturn Johnny Thomson might sometimes match Jimmy

rimming Langhorne. Jimmy, nevertheless, was grand master.

We've already gone into how he and his trademark *Dean Van Lines* unhinged the racing of the 1950s. Jimmy's dominance was a matter of unleashing a new strategy based on aggression, intimidation, superhuman discipline, complete lack of fear in traffic, and a fanatical obsession for rough surfaces and for Langhonre. "The Walking Ox" was what continentals had called Bryan after he'd gone to Italy and blown them sideways at Monza's Race of Two Worlds. Although meant as an insult, the tag was apt. He did have the stamina to carry a fractured car home on his broad back and still win, as he and the disintegrating *Dean* nearly

"There are no bad race tracks, only bad race drivers," believed Bobby Grim, four-time seasonal champion of the IMCA cornstalk circuit. Bobby, however, usually avoided Langhorne.
Bob Tronolone

Race Driver of the Century Mario Andretti ahead of two other stragglers, was able to squeeze the Langhorne 100 of 1964 into his itinerary—the last before the big black circle was paved.
Bruce Craig

did on the bricks of Indy in 1954 when they'd seemed to be overcoming Vukovich.

And what about Jimmy at his home crucible Phoenix in 1957? After either getting crowded off the groove or just losing it, he left the track—literally disappearing through a hole in the fence—and just when everybody thought they'd seen the last of him this time, he reentered the race bringing lumber with him. Winning, he pulled his "Look Ma, no hands," celebration stunt of throwing both mitts into the sky, one of many Jimmy trademarks. Always keeping a long unlit cigar clamped in his mouth was another, and the infantile bad-boy act of throwing firecrackers was yet another.

Jimmy had so many hard miles on him he looked older, but he was only 33 when Langhorne took him down. Born in Phoenix, he left as a teenager to get in on World War II. The same old story. Many unreconstructed warriors took up racing following the armistice,

and Jimmy, who emerged from the Air Force with his wings despite being only a kid, was among them.

He was a natural; a few monster races in midgets and sprint cars were all he needed to get going. One occurred at Fresno, home of Vookie and all his irascible relatives. Vookie stuffed a wheel up to elbow Jimmy, and Jimmy, in an unthinking, automatic response, did the same thing in retaliation. Afterward, when Vook presented himself, apparently preparing to brawl, Jimmy was ready to fight in return, even if he had to take on every Vukovich in Fresno. He received hearty congratulations instead.

Jimmy next brought a dirt-rubbered purple rail job midget with a handbrake to Cincinnati Bowl and used three of four dirt track tires—the only kind he'd brought with him—to almost beat the gang. Only the pavement tire failed. Then he breezed into Williams Grove, which Hinnershitz in those days guarded like a fortress, and in a sprinter threw an impossible outside maneuver on Tommy good enough to win. Cramming himself back into a midget on the DuQuoin mile, Jimmy made a spectacle exploding from 31st hole to 3rd.

But midgets, sprints, and even taxicabs weren't Jimmy's medium: his genius broke loose when he started shaking down big 270 Offy champ cars, in which he would surpass even mile-track monarch Tony Bettenhausen. His initial championship win came in 1953, when he won the 100 miles of Sacramento for Bessie Lee Paoli, but Jimmy's real story began in 1954 when the Dean Van Lines recruited him to race its Kuzma.

Officially the Dean outfit belonged to Al Dean, a sportsman and rake from the Bel Aire martini and country club circuit. But the team's true boss was its pistol of a chief mechanic Brawner. Just like it had Jimmy, dirt racing had already ravaged Clint beyond his years. Further, his explosive temper and blaring voice stampeded racing officials, stewards, and especially drivers. Like Don Shepherd with Bobby Unser and Wally Meskowski with A. J. Foyt, Johnny Rutherford and Mario Andretti, Clint was hard to impress, yet he was fully aware of the caliber of race driver he had in Jimmy and would do anything for him.

Once, when Jimmy appeared to be getting cheated because of a yellow flag, Clint, choleric, tried physically assaulting three stewards at once. A DuQuoin race that Bryan was clearly losing to Sweikert ended instead in yet another Jimmy victory, when Clint brought out his book of dirty tricks to torment his former driver and do Sweikert in with a trick signal. Another time at DuQuoin when Jimmy was practicing and got the *Dean* upside-down, Clint got the rule rescinded about a flipped car not getting to race and Jimmy won yet again.

The only other time I have been able to determine that this happened was with sprint cars at Williams Grove when Wally and A. J. buffaloed the stewards identically. And in 1955 at Langhorne when rain interrupted the 100 for a week, all the dirt camp cars were supposed to be put under lock and key so no maintenance could be performed on them. But the *Dean* had a valve going out, Clint again thwarted the rules, and Jimmy won the following Sunday with the *Dean* performing like a juggernaut.

That score was Jimmy's second Langhorne in a row, something nobody had ever done before, and nobody could raise the hot-blooded Langhorne faithful like Jimmy. In 1956 he made his amazing move for three straight. After qualifying what for him was a poor fifth, by 16 miles he was leading and by 42 had the field lapped. But the *Dean's* fuel tank was leaking and at 70 miles Jimmy had to stop. Clint was slow topping Jimmy up, but they both caught a break because of a yellow flag that let Jimmy come out of the pits third. He had 19 miles to make up a deficit of a lap and 30 seconds. Get outta the way!

"Bryan's driving after he turned over the lead was indescribable," reported Jim Lunt, who tried anyway. "The laps after he left the pits were the greatest I have ever seen Bryan turn in. He passed inside, outside, and went between cars fighting for position to make it three abreast . . . The crowd was cheering him on as he kept gaining and gaining."

First he unlapped the entire field, then commenced relapping it, and had closed the lead down to half a lap with nine miles to go when he had to stop for more fuel.

"Jimmy," concluded Jim, "took the loss with the usual stoical attitude." Perhaps. Clint, on the other hand, did not. For once it was a chief mechanic, not a driver, who had fear in his heart. Watching Jimmy hang his hide out that way and even ignore pleading signals to slow down had twisted Clint's belly into an excruciating knot and through the last miles he'd been unable to watch Jimmy at all. Clint, ostensibly hard-baited, was in reality a sentimental basket case. Vowing not to be the chief mechanic who wiped out the great Bryan, Clint told his man he was never bringing him back, and if he still wanted to race at Langhorne he'd better do it with somebody else.

So Jimmy missed out on the opportunity to win as many Langhornes as his 'Horne successor A. J. would. But in 1958, following six previous failures there, Jimmy at least got lucky at Indy and won the 500. To do so, unfortunately, he'd had to abandon Clint and Dean Van Lines and race for another team. Clint never fully forgave him.

And then—too late—Jimmy realized he had outsmarted himself. For years the Indy 500 winner had been expected to be a racing champion and go on competing. But the wholesale destruction of Sweikert, and the serious wounds to Lee Wallard, Troy Ruttman, and Pat Flaherty now argued that the 500 winner be unofficially sentenced to the agony of semiretirement. He was expected to climb off the devouring dirt and go enjoy his big payday. And sure enough, for 1958 and 1959 Jimmy played that game by accepting accolades and commercial endorsements and making himself a model winner, hitting the banquet circuit to mouth

May 1, 1955, was Mike Nazarak's end. Here (above), he comes around the outside to win his qualifying heat; (right) zeroes in on leader Charlie Musselman in the main event; gains the lead (opposite, top) and pulls away, only to crash and get thrown out; and (opposite, bottom) the driverless *Nyquist* Offy comes to rest, burning on its wheels. *Bruce Craig*

goodwill ambassador speeches. Happy at racing, a mess when not, he also made himself miserable. By 1960 he was seeking serious action again.

Jimmy's opportunity to return to Langhorne came about in the most innocent and casual way imaginable. During an otherwise routine boozy June night at the bar of the Holiday Inn across from the Brickyard, A. J. Watson came walking out of the gents' just as Jimmy came walking in. Knowing that Ward wasn't going to, Jimmy asked A. J., "Who's going to run your dirt car at Langhorne?" And A. J. automatically replied, "You are."

Rodger was horrified when he heard—he tried but failed to argue Jimmy out of it.

One thing was sure. On that last afternoon of his life, Jimmy still knew his way around the 'Horne; his time trial lap was second-quick and parked him on the outside of the front row. On the other hand, he'd been away for so long that he scarcely knew the moves of Branson, Herkie, Upside-Down, and Jim Packard, the main opposition he faced. But all four knew what a great target Jimmy made and set aim accordingly.

Jimmy's accident was blamed on Jimmy. But it was also variously attributed to Don's *Bob Estes* brushing Jimmy's *Leader Card*—or maybe it had been Herkie in the *Schmidt*. Or maybe a *Leader Card* tire went flat or possibly the front suspension of the *Leader Card* fell apart. In any case, Langhorne had struck again.

Back in Indianapolis at the White Front, just to make everyone feel bad, a mawkish dirge complete with Offy sounds called "The Ballad of Jimmy Bryan" became the new jukebox favorite. Jimmy had been a White Front regular. On nights in the famous watering hole when it was so crowded he couldn't find a place to sit down, jovial Jimbo had been in the habit of clearing a table for himself by heaving a counterfeit M80 firecracker in its direction, making the occupants bolt. If they still wouldn't, the next banger tossed would be the real thing: KA-BLAM!

Firecrackering went out of fashion after 1960, and so did throwing both mitts into the sky—those had been Jimmy's stunts. A. J., Jimmy's successor, did take a shot at mitt-throwing in 1961, after A. J. won his first Hoosier Hundred. It was a race Jimmy won three successive years, and perhaps A. J. meant it in tribute. But the first corner was rutty, and after receiving the checkered, A. J. drove into some of the ruts while still mimicking Jimmy's no-hands signature and almost wore it. A. J. never tried it again.

Master A. J.

Symbolically, after Jimmy had gone elsewhere in 1958 and Clint and Dean Van Lines needed somebody new to put in Bryan's classic Kuzma, they picked young A. J., whose big career move subsequently occurred at Langhorne. He was still in the Brawner doghouse after spinning out at Indy just two weeks earlier, but A. J. redeemed himself to Clint by making a last-gasp 'Horne pass of Jud Larson for second place. That started things off. Stamping his identity on Langhorne just as much as he did every place else, A. J., between 1961–1964, carried off a record-four 'Horne champ car scores.

His own ascendancy was accompanied by George Bignotti's coascendancy as boss of chief mechanics. Just as A. J. as a driver ultimately surpassed Jimmy, so George eventually eclipsed Clint.

At that same 1958 Langhorne where A. J. overtook Jud, George had to observe his own burning *Bowes Seal Fast* Lesovsky melting to cinders on the back-straight. Now he needed a new driver to replace the injured Johnny Boyd, so for George it was fortuitous timing when Jud Larson—perturbed at A. J. Watson for not flashing a signal warning that Foyt was preparing to pounce—subsequently announced a career move from racing back to selling junk heaps at Pancho Alvarez's.

But George persuaded Jud that he still had racing left in him, and sure enough Jud did, because he won George and Bowes Seal Fast the big clash at Phoenix that fall. George retained him for 1959, but with no wins, and Jud's health was slipping, so at the end of the year George moved in on Foyt, who had grown dissatisfied with Clint and Dean Van Lines. Five years later, A. J. and George at last became terminally dissatisfied with each other, too, but not before they'd made themselves the great driver-mechanic duo of 1951–1971.

At Langhorne they were always especially tough: damn near invincible. In 1961's 100 A. J. and the *Bowes Seal Fast* Meskowski won by a whole lap over Parnelli, and in 1962's July 100 A. J. looked like Jimmy by dominating and leading every mile. In 1962 USAC sadistically scheduled two Langhornes in one year, and in the second match in August Don Branson won and set the eternal Langhorne record average of 104.799 miles per hour at the wheel of the same old *Leonard Card 1* that had done in Jimmy. (A. J., who was on the outs with George at this race, qualified a Hopkins Special quickest, then blistered a right rear at 33 miles—something that would never happen to him again when he was back in harness with George at Sheraton-Thompson.)

Jimmy Bryan. *Russ Reed, Scalzo collection*

An especially big year for A. J. at Langhorne was 1963, when he won a sprinter feature of 50 miles in April, a taxicab meet in May, and the champ car 100 in June. In the last race, A. J. finally took some hits. Competition was falling off, and the 'Horne could muster just 14 starters, but Bobby Marshman that year was not ready to concede A. J. was fastest. From sixth hole he took off hard, and at 28 miles Bobby was checking out on A. J. and everyone.

But the old Marshman dilemma of not having an oversize neck to accommodate his size-13 foot took over, and poor pencil Bobby couldn't hold his head upright any longer; worn out, he had to cede the throne of the *Hopkins* Meskowski to Branson. A. J., meanwhile, was winning yet again and lapping everyone up to third place in his own *Sheraton-Thompson* Meskowski.

Then in 1964, A. J. received his newer, even faster, Meskowki and won Springfield, DuQuoin, the Hoosier Hundred, and Sacramento, besides his fourth Langhorne. Young Johnny Rutherford was there, and had met one of his own goals by winning a Langhorne pole. Aged Jud Larson was there, chipping away at A. J. for joining the other sissies racing on dirt with power steering. But Johnny and his *J. H. Rose* Chevy couldn't touch A. J. once the racing started. And after A. J.'s unit tanked in the middle of the show and A. J. had to cover the last 50 miles with no power steering, yet still won at an average speed faster than he qualified, there was no more Jud chatter about sissies.

A. J. was the only Langhorne personality that you could watch without ever worrying that the 'Horne would eat him up. Certainly not with George there maintaining the *Bowes Seal Fast* and Sheraton Thompson

Bryan's Langhorne 100 scores of 1954 and 1955 were huge, and his near-win in 1956 was epic, but the drive of his life may well have occurred at the Phoenix mile of 1957, when in order to win, Jimmy had to knock down a fence. Here he recuperates. *Jack Fox, Scalzo collection*

hardware just so. A. J. never looked in danger from the 'Horne—A. J. tamed the 'Horne.

June 2, 1957

Langhorne being the ultimate dirt track, it followed that perhaps the ultimate performance by a dirt driver of 1951–1971 should also occur there. The hero pulling it off was Johnny Thomson. Not even Jimmy Bryan had previously come very close to the unrecognized dream of covering the hellish 100 miles of Langhorne in under an hour. Going that fast was a distant legacy of the board track school, when the flying Duesies and supercharged Millers were achieving it only because they were competing on the looming bankings of timber bowls. But on June 2, 1957, Johnny and that super-Kuzma, the *D-A Lubricants*, pulled it off at the 'Horne with six seconds to spare.

Just two years afterward, in late summer of 1959, the White Front, Gasoline Alley, and other intelligence bazaars were crackling over the controversial news that Herk Hurtubise with his dazzling eyes and wrecker reputation was going to get a rookie shot as temporary

Bryan owed Jud Larson, here, a case of beer in thanks for what Jud did inadvertently at the 1957 Phoenix. Making a mistake, Jud swerved off the mile and left behind a hole that he punched through the outside fence. Later crowded off the track in the same exact place, Jimmy used Jud's old hole to exit, then re-enter, the track, and go on to win. *Bob Tronolone*

replacement driver for the *Racing Associates* Kuzma, the former *D-A Lubricants*. Predictions flew a dime a dozen that this was a terrible mistake, bound to end in a typical Hurtubise crash-'n'-burn. Only laid-back Jud Larson saw the ironic humor of all the dire predictions. Jud laughingly drawled, "Listen, the guy Hurtubise is replacing didn't get hurt at Williams Grove while he was mowing the lawn!"

No, he certainly hadn't. The hurt guy was Johnny Thomson, Langhorne's ace but also dirt's most infamous serial crasher, and at the Grove it hadn't been a lawn mower but a race car—a flipping sprinter—that had scuffed him up, again.

Johnny's timing was embarrassing and typical. His long-suffering fans had previously scheduled a Johnny Thomson Day of Appreciation at Reading, with Jim Lunt coming in as celebrity host. But the Williams Grove flip occurred just the week before, so Johnny executed the characteristic reversal of going from man-of-the-hour to damaged goods, resting in the emergency ward too busted up to come to Reading for his own Day of Appreciation.

He was a difficult one, Johnny. Bryan, Larson, Nazaruk, Sweikert, and so many others of the 1951–1971 cast who were carried off, rank as greats because they all raced at the limits of their skills without crashing—the only big wreck any of them ever had was the one that killed them. Yet Johnny Thomson, who was inferior to none of the four in skill, and who was 100-mile speed record holder not just at Langhorne but Syracuse, Springfield, DuQuoin, and Sacramento, had a such a hard-crashing time throughout his six big tournaments of 1955 through 1960 that his career seemed like one long kamikaze run ending with his final sprint car ride that September.

Like Mike Nazaruk, Johnny came out of World War II with various decorations attesting to his bravery beyond the call of duty. Car owners and chief mechanics were always telling their drivers to stand on the gas as hard as that Johnny Thomson, leading to many hair-standing anecdotes, including these two.

Syracuse, 1956: The 18 starters at the 100 were paced by a dingaling on the pole who acted like he was reading a road map while bringing everyone to the green at a crawl and provoking a huge traffic bottleneck. Three rows behind, Johnny in the *D-A* on the inside and Smokey Elisian in the *John Zink* on the outside were grumbling to themselves: "this balloon-foot crap isn't getting us anywhere, we're comin'!" Johnny

At Langhorne and the Hoosier Hundred, Eddie Sachs treated the noble *Peter Schmidt* Kuzma to two of its five career wins. *Bob Tronolone*

A. J. Foyt was the one player from the 1951–1971 dirt track cast who seemed immune from danger at the 'Horne.
Bob Tronolone

cut left, Smokey right. And while Johnny was blowing off the four automobiles ahead of him on the inside, Smokey was doing the identical thing outside. Neither driver was aware that the other was there until they both popped clean at the same time and arrived into the first corner dead-heated for first and poised to crack up the whole field if either of them blinked. Dead ahead was the typically hard and narrow Syracuse corner groove with no room for accommodating two side-by-side champ cars.

Smokey was one of the few dumb enough or brave enough to take on Johnny, so they took the plunge together, still deadlocked, Johnny still inside, Smokey outside. Johnny subsequently moved ahead down the back-straight, yet on this day Smokey earned all kinds of points for refusing to cave and for being able to

negotiate one and two corners holding himself level with Johnny Thomson. Had Smokey only been able to conduct his business that cleanly at the Indy 500 two years later, he and Dick Rathmann might not have had their first-lap catastrophe.

Langhorne, 1959: Seeing that his driver A. J. Foyt had the *Dean Van Lines* lined up just behind Johnny in the *Racing Associates*, Clint Brawner instructed A. J. to tag on and follow him as best he could. But the advice backfired when Johnny, having another of his tough days, couldn't get the *D-A* turned. He hit a wall and ruined a tire; had to stop for a new one, then came back and crashed all over again. "Don't you ever tell me to follow *that* guy again," A. J. pleaded afterward, and, upon hearing what A. J. had said, Johnny permitted himself a rueful laugh. But the joke was on Johnny as

usual because laughing made him feel the pair of ribs he'd cracked. At least it was just two. In a 1955 roller at Langhorne with the *Peter Schmidt* he broke five and suffered shoulder fractures.

Still, Johnny did score the big moment for which many a fellow dirt iron from 1951–1971 might have traded a career.

June 2, 1957, at Langhorne came just three days after the Indy 500 and almost three-quarters of the 500 starters were boycotting the 'Horne as usual. Johnny had spun

out at Indy but for one of the relatively few times in his black-and-blue existence was totally sound physically.

So away another Langhorne 100 went, and Johnny, from pole, shot straight into the lead and lapped his first straggler in three miles. By 11, he'd doubled 10. By 25 just three were left to vanquish, including Jud Larson and Eddie Sachs. By 41, they, too, were history. But then Johnny popped the right rear and had to make a forced rubber stop; while he was in the process of spinning around in the pits getting stopped, some wit

Just one last time. A. J. and the *Sheraton-Thompson* Meskowski, the ultimate driver/car combo of the dirt track 1960s. *Bob Tronolone*

Johnny Thomson wins the 1958 Sacramento 100. *Bob Tronolone*

A. J. trails Jud at the 1965 Sacramento. But possibly the biggest career move A. J. ever made occurred at the 'Horne in 1959 when he surprised Jud on the last lap and passed him for runner-up money and glory. *Bob Tronolone*

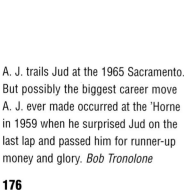

observed that that was the only right-hand turn he'd made all day.

To get back into the lead again, Johnny had to top Bryan's from-the-back Langhorne binge of 1956, and perhaps exceed even his own 'Horne talents as well. He did. What was everyone else's corner became Johnny's straightaway—he was masterful. Eddie Sachs couldn't repel Johnny and gave way. Johnny's final obstacle, Jud Larson, tried to, but went on his head. Cleaning up the mess and attending to Jud ate up half a dozen yellow-flag miles. Barely four laps of green-flag racing remained as Johnny resumed the coup de main, and there's never been anything like it.

Drivers who were racing that day afterward said that dust was so thick they couldn't see through their own windshields yet upstairs, high on the rim, they could hear Johnny hard on the pedal moving the dirt and going Roar! Roar! Roar!

Posterity has recorded that on the 99th mile a rare summer storm broke out over Langhorne; and precisely as Johnny caught the checkered, a single clap of thunder was heard. Emergency stop notwithstanding, Johnny had sped through the century in six seconds less than an hour.

With Johnny, of course, good fortune never lasted. Within months he injured himself badly at Sacramento;

Bad Man's finest hour—actually 59 minutes and 56 seconds—of June 1, 1957. *Bruce Craig*

and recovered in 1958 to be fast all over again and win Springfield, DuQuoin, Syracuse and Sacramento. Then he got rebusted at Williams Grove in 1959; in 1960 at Allentown, on a track surface so vile that even the trotting horse gentry had refused to send their jugheads and men onto it, Johnny became another of the big-player statistics while racing the same sprinter that had done in Bill Schindler on the same track eight years before. Dirt stories don't come much sadder than Johnny Thomson's.

Johnny's nickname was "Bad Man"—the ultimate handle for perhaps dirt tracking's ultimate driver. As might be expected, it came from Sam Traylor, who thought Thomson's red protective face bandana made him look like a brigand. Johnny was a 5-foot-something, 150-pound exception to Langhorne's big foot and neck law. Recalled today as almost grimly antisocial, let's hope that Johnny—the 'Horne's record-setting, history-provoking conqueror—walked off the battle-ground in the Langhorne rain, for once, as deliriously happy as everyone else, because June 1, 1957, was the whole 1951–1971 dirt track experience writ huge.

Keep standing on it, rim-riding that Langhorne lip forever, Bad Man.

INDEX

U.S.A.C.

A. J. FOYT

JIM HU

A FULL FIELD OF INDY '500' STARS FR

FRIDAY NITE